Grade 2

Comprehension
and Critical
Thinking

- ✓ Test Preparation
- ✓ Comprehension and Critical Thinking Questions
- ✓ Document-Based Analysis

Author

Lisa Greathouse

The articles in this book are collected from the TIME For Kids archives.

SHELL EDUCATION

Editor
Jodene Lynn Smith, M.A.

Compiler
Maria Elvira Gallardo, M.A.

Assistant Editor
Leslie Huber, M.A.

Katie Das

Editorial Director
Dona Herweck Rice

Editor-in-Chief
Sharon Coan, M.S.Ed.

Editorial Manager
Gisela Lee, M.A.

Creative Director
Lee Aucoin

Cover Image
Compilation from
shutterstock.com

Illustration Manager
Timothy J. Bradley

Artist
Mira Fraser

Interior Layout Designer
Don Tran

Publisher
Corinne Burton, M.A.Ed.

Standards Compendium, Copyright 2004 McREL

Shell Education
5301 Oceanus Drive
Huntington Beach, CA 92649-1030
http://www.shelleducation.com
ISBN 978-1-4258-0242-4
© 2008 Shell Educational Publishing, Inc.
Reprinted 2012

Table of Contents

Introduction and Research

Comprehension is the primary goal of any reading task. According to the RAND Reading Study Group, comprehension is "the process of simultaneously extracting and constructing meaning through interaction and involvement with written language" (2002, 11). Students who comprehend what they read have more opportunities in life, as well as better test performance. In order for students to become proficient readers, it is necessary that they are taught comprehension strategies such as predicting, monitoring comprehension, summarizing, visualizing, questioning, making connections, and inferring meaning (Miller 2002; Pardo 2002).

Focus on reading comprehension has become more urgent in light of NCLB legislation and emphasis on standardized testing. Because the majority of text found on standardized tests is nonfiction (Grigg, Daane, Jin, & Campbell 2003), teachers are now finding a greater need to teach skills using informational texts. For this reason, *Comprehension and Critical Thinking* provides teachers with informational texts in the form of articles about the contemporary world, as well as the past.

Research suggests that students need preparation in order to be successful on standardized tests. Gulek states: "Adequate and appropriate test preparation plays an important role in helping students demonstrate their knowledge and skills in high-stakes testing situations" (2003, 42). This preparation includes, among other things, teaching content and test-taking skills. Skills practiced when using the articles in *Comprehension and Critical Thinking* provide an excellent foundation for improving students' test-taking abilities.

Not only is reading nonfiction texts beneficial for testing purposes, but studies also show that students actually prefer informational texts. A 1998 study by Kletzien that focused on children's preferences for reading material indicated that younger children chose nonfiction text close to half the time when choosing their own reading materials. Similar studies (Ivey & Broaddus 2000; Moss & Hendershot 2002) revealed that older children prefer nonfiction and find greater motivation when reading informational texts.

In this book, each nonfiction passage includes a document-based question similar to trends in standardized testing. The students respond to a critical-thinking question based on the information gleaned from a given document. This document is related to the passage it accompanies. Document-based questions show a student's ability to apply prior knowledge and his or her capacity to transfer knowledge to a new situation. The activities are time efficient, allowing students to practice these skills every week. To yield the best results, such practice must begin at the start of the school year.

Students will need to use test-taking skills and strategies throughout their lives. The exercises in *Comprehension and Critical Thinking* will guide your students to become better readers and test takers. After practicing the exercises in this book, you will be pleased with your students' comprehension performance not only on standardized tests, but also with any expository text they encounter within the classroom and beyond its walls.

Introduction and Research (cont.)

Objectives

All lessons in this book are designed to support the following objectives.

The students will:

- answer who, what, where, why, when, and how questions about the article
- support answers with information found in the article
- support answers with information inferred from the article
- support answers with information based on prior knowledge
- identify the main ideas in the article
- identify supporting details in the article
- draw conclusions based on information learned in the article
- make predictions based on information learned in the article
- form and defend an opinion based on information learned in the article
- respond to questions in written form

Readability

All of the reading passages included in this book have a 2.0–2.9 reading level based on the Flesch-Kincaid Readability Formula. This formula determines a readability level by calculating the number of words, syllables, and sentences.

Preparing Students to Read Nonfiction Text

One of the best ways to prepare students to read expository text is to read a short selection aloud daily. Reading expository text aloud is critical to developing your students' abilities to read it themselves. Because making predictions is another way to help students tap into their prior knowledge, read the beginning of a passage, then stop and ask the students to predict what might occur next. Do this at several points throughout your reading of the text. By doing this over time, you will find that your students' abilities to make accurate predictions greatly increases.

Of course, talking about nonfiction concepts is also very important. However, remember that discussion can never replace actually reading nonfiction texts because people rarely speak using the vocabulary and complex sentence structures of written language.

Asking questions helps students, especially struggling readers, to focus on what is important in a text. Also, remember the significance of wait time. Research has shown that the amount of time an educator waits for a student to answer after posing a question has a critical effect on learning. So, after you ask a student a question, silently count to five (or ten, if you have a student who struggles to get his or her thoughts into words) before giving any additional prompts or redirecting the question to another student.

© Shell Education   #50242—Comprehension and Critical Thinking   5

Bloom's Taxonomy

The questions that follow each passage in *Comprehension and Critical Thinking* assess all levels of learning by following Bloom's Taxonomy, a six-level classification system for comprehension questions that was devised by Benjamin Bloom in 1956. The questions that follow each passage are always presented in order, progressing from *knowledge* to *evaluation*.

The skills listed for each level are essential to keep in mind when teaching comprehension in order to assure that your students reach the higher levels of thinking. Use this classification to form your own questions whenever your students listen to or read material.

Level 1: Knowledge—Students recall information or find requested information in an article. They show memory of dates, events, places, people, and main ideas.

Level 2: Comprehension—Students understand information. This means that they can find information that is stated in a different way from how the question is presented. It also means that students can rephrase or restate information in their own words.

Level 3: Application—Students apply their knowledge to a specific situation. They may be asked to do something new with the knowledge.

Level 4: Analysis—Students break things into components and examine those parts. They notice patterns in information.

Level 5: Synthesis—Students do something new with the information. They pull knowledge together to create new ideas. They generalize, predict, plan, and draw conclusions.

Level 6: Evaluation—Students make judgments and assess value. They form an opinion and defend it. They can also understand another person's viewpoint.

Practice Suggestions: Multiple-Choice Questions

Complete the first three passages and related questions with the whole class. Demonstrate your own metacognitive processes by thinking aloud about how to figure out an answer. This means that you essentially tell your students your thoughts as they come to you. For example, suppose the question is the following: "In a national park, bears a) roam free, b) stay in cages, or c) get caught in traps." Tell the students all your thoughts as they occur to you, for example: "Well, the article was about bears living in national parks. It didn't mention that they stay in cages. They probably only do that in zoos or circuses. So, I'll get rid of that choice. That leaves me with the choices *roam free* or *get caught in traps*. Let me look back at the article and see what it says about traps. (Refer to the article.) I don't see anything about traps in the passage, and I do see that it says that in national parks, the bears are safe. That means they're safe from traps, which are dangerous. So I'm going to select *roam free*." As students hear the thought process you go through as you determine answers to questions, they will begin to apply the same strategies as they go to answer questions.

Introduction and Research _(cont.)

Practice Suggestions: Short-Answer Questions

The short-answer question for each passage is evaluative—the highest level of Bloom's Taxonomy. It is basically an opinion statement with no definitive right answer. The students are asked to take stances and defend them. While there is no correct response, it is critical to show the students how to support their opinions using facts and logic. Show the students a format for a response—state their opinion followed by the word *because* and a reason. For example, "I do not think that whales should be kept at sea parks because they are wild animals and don't want to be there. They want to be in the ocean with their friends." Do not award credit unless the child adequately supports his or her conclusion. Before passing back the practice papers, make note of two children who had opposing opinions. Then, during the discussion, call on each of these students to read his or her short-answer response to the class. (If all the children drew the same conclusion, come up with support for the opposing one yourself.)

Practice Suggestions: Document-Based Questions

It is especially important to guide your students in how to understand, interpret, and respond to the document-based questions. For these questions, in order to formulate a response, the students will have to rely on their prior knowledge and common sense in addition to the information provided in the document. Again, the best way to teach this is to demonstrate through thinking aloud how to figure out an answer. Since these questions are usually interpretive, you can allow for some variation in student responses.

The more your students practice, the more competent and confident they will become. Plan to have the class do every exercise in *Comprehension and Critical Thinking*. If you have some students who cannot read the articles independently, allow them to read with partners, and then work through the comprehension questions alone. Eventually, all students must practice reading and answering the questions independently. Move to this stage as soon as possible. For the most effective practice sessions, follow these steps:

1. Have the students read the text silently and answer the questions.

2. Have the students exchange papers to correct each other's multiple-choice section.

3. Collect all the papers to score the short-answer question and the document-based question portion.

4. Return the papers to their owners and discuss how the students determined their answers.

5. Refer to the exact wording in the passage.

6. Point out how students had to use their background knowledge to answer certain questions.

7. Discuss how a student should explain his or her stance in each short-answer question.

8. Discuss the document-based question thoroughly.

Introduction and Research (cont.)

Scoring the Practice Passages

Identify the number of correct responses when scoring the practice passages. Share the number of correct responses with the students. This is the number they will most easily identify; additionally, the number of correct responses coincides with the Student Achievement Graph. However, for your own records and to share with the parents, you may want to keep track of numeric scores for each student. If you choose to do this, do not write the numeric score on the paper.

To generate a numeric score, follow these guidelines:

Type of Question	Number of Questions	Points Possible Per Question	Total Number of Points
Multiple-choice questions	6	10 points each	60 points
Short-answer question	1	15 points	15 points
Document-based question	1	25 points	25 points
Total			100 points

Standardized Test Success

One of the key objectives of *Comprehension and Critical Thinking* is to prepare your students to get the best possible scores on the reading portion of standardized tests. A student's ability to do well on traditional standardized tests in comprehension requires these factors:

- a large vocabulary
- test-taking skills
- the ability to cope with stress effectively

Every student in your class needs instruction in test-taking skills. Even fluent readers and logical thinkers will perform better on standardized tests if you provide instruction in the following areas:

Understanding the question—Teach the students how to break down the question to figure out what is really being asked. This book will prepare the students for the kinds of questions they will encounter on standardized tests.

Concentrating only on what the text says—Show the students how to restrict their responses to only what is asked. When you review the practice passages, ask your students to show where they found the correct response in the text.

Ruling out distracters in multiple-choice answers—Teach the students to look for the key words in a question and look for those specific words to find the information in the text. They also need to know that they may have to look for synonyms for the key words.

Maintaining concentration—Use classroom time to practice this in advance. Reward the students for maintaining concentration. Explain to them the purpose of this practice and the reason why concentration is so essential.

Teaching Nonfiction Comprehension Skills

Nonfiction comprehension encompasses many skills that develop with a lot of practice. The following information offers a brief overview the crucial skills of recognizing text structure, visualizing, summarizing, and learning new vocabulary. This information is designed for use with other classroom materials, not the practice passages in *Comprehension and Critical Thinking*.

Many of these skills can be found in scope-and-sequence charts and standards for reading comprehension:

- recognizes the main idea
- identifies details
- determines sequence
- recalls details
- labels parts
- summarizes
- identifies time sequence
- describes character(s)
- retells information in own words

- classifies, sorts into categories
- compares and contrasts
- makes generalizations
- draws conclusions
- recognizes text organization
- predicts outcome and consequences
- experiences an emotional reaction to a text
- recognizes facts
- applies information to a new situation

Typical Comprehension Questions

Teaching the typical kinds of standardized-test questions gives students an anticipation framework and helps them learn how to comprehend what they read. It also boosts their test scores. Questions generally found on standardized reading comprehension tests are as follows:

Facts—questions based on what the text states: who, what, when, where, why, and how

Sequence—questions based on order: what happened first, last, and in between

Conditions—questions asking the students to compare, contrast, and find the similarities and differences

Summarizing—questions that require the students to restate, paraphrase, choose main ideas, conclude, and select a title

Vocabulary—questions based on word meaning, synonyms and antonyms, proper nouns, words in context, technical words, geographical words, and unusual adjectives

Outcomes—questions that ask readers to draw upon their own experiences or prior knowledge, which means that students must understand cause and effect, consequences, and implications

Opinion—questions that ask the author's intent and require the use of inference skills

Document-based—questions that require students to analyze information from a source document to draw a conclusion or form an opinion

Teaching Nonfiction Comprehension Skills (cont.)

Teaching Text Structure

Students lacking in knowledge of text structure are at a distinct disadvantage, yet this skill is sometimes overlooked in instruction. When referring to a text to locate information to answer a question, understanding structure allows students to quickly locate the right area in which to look. The students also need to understand text structure in order to make predictions and improve overall comprehension.

Some students have been so immersed in print that they have a natural understanding of structure. For instance, they realize that the first sentence of a paragraph often contains the main idea, followed by details about that idea. But many students need direct instruction in text structure. The first step in this process is making certain that students know the way that authors typically present ideas in writing. This knowledge is a major asset for students.

Transitional paragraphs join together two paragraphs to make the writing flow. Most transitional paragraphs do not have a main idea. In all other paragraph types, there is a main idea, even if it is not stated. In the following examples, the main idea is italicized. In order of frequency, the four types of expository paragraph structures are as follows:

1. **The main idea is often the first sentence of a paragraph. The rest of the paragraph provides the supporting details.**

   Clara Barton, known as America's first nurse, was a brave and devoted humanitarian. While caring for others, she was shot at, got frostbitten fingers, and burned her hands. She had severe laryngitis twice and almost lost her eyesight. Yet she continued to care for the sick and injured until she died at the age of 91.

2. **The main idea may fall in the center of the paragraph, surrounded on both sides by details.**

   The coral has created a reef where more than 200 kinds of birds and about 1,500 types of fish live. *In fact, Australia's Great Barrier Reef provides a home for many interesting animals.* These include sea turtles, giant clams, crabs, and crown-of-thorns starfish.

3. **The main idea comes at the end of the paragraph as a summary of the details that came before.**

   Each year, Antarctica spends six months in darkness, from mid-March to mid-September. The continent is covered year-round by ice, which causes sunlight to reflect off its surface. It never really warms up. In fact, the coldest temperature ever recorded was in Antarctica. *Antarctica has one of the harshest environments in the world.*

4. **The main idea is not stated in the paragraph and must be inferred from the details given. This paragraph structure is the most challenging for primary students.**

   The biggest sea horse ever found was over a foot long. Large sea horses live along the coasts of New Zealand, Australia, and California. Smaller sea horses live off the coast of Florida, in the Caribbean Sea, and in the Gulf of Mexico. The smallest adult sea horse ever found was only one-half inch long!

   In this example, the implied main idea is that sea horses' sizes vary based on where they live.

Teaching Nonfiction Comprehension Skills (cont.)

Teaching Text Structure (cont.)

Some other activities that will help your students understand text structure include the following:

Color code—While reading a text, have the students use different-colored pencils or highlighters to color-code important elements such as the main idea (red), supporting details (yellow), causes (green) and effects (purple), and facts (blue) and opinions (orange). When they have finished, ask them to describe the paragraph's structure in their own words.

Search the text—Teach the students to identify the key words in a question and look specifically for those words in the passage. Then, when you discuss a comprehension question with the students, ask them, "Which words will you look for in the text to find the answer? If you can't find the words, can you find synonyms? Where will you look for the words?"

Signal words—There are specific words used in text that indicate, or signal, that the text has a cause-effect, sequence, or comparison structure. Teaching your students these words will greatly improve their abilities to detect text structure and increase their comprehension.

These Signal Words	Indicate
since, because, caused by, as a result, before and after, so, this led to, if/then, reasons, brought about, so that, when/then, that's why	cause and effect The answer to "Why did it happen?" is a cause. The answer to "What happened?" is an effect.
first, second, third, next, then, after, before, last, later, since then, now, while, meanwhile, at the same time, finally, when, at last, in the end, since that time, following, on (date), at (time)	sequence
but, even if, even though, although, however, instead, not only, unless, yet, on the other hand, either/or, as well as, "–er" and "–st" words (such as better, best, shorter, tallest, bigger, smallest, most, worst)	compare/contrast

Teaching Visualization Skills

Visualization—Visualization is seeing the words of a text as mental images. It is a significant factor that sets apart proficient readers from low-achieving ones. Studies have shown that the ability to generate vivid images while reading strongly correlates with a person's comprehension of text. However, research has also revealed that 20 percent of all children do not visualize or experience sensory images when reading. These children are thus handicapped in their ability to comprehend text, and they are usually the students who avoid and dislike reading because they never connect to text in a personal, meaningful way.

Active visualization can completely engross a reader in text. You have experienced this when you just could not put a book down and you stayed up all night just to finish it. Skilled readers automatically weave their own memories into text as they read to make personalized, lifelike images. In fact, every person develops a unique interpretation of any text. This personalized reading experience explains why most people prefer a book to its movie.

Visualization is not static; unlike photographs, these are "movies in the mind." Mental images must constantly be modified to incorporate new information as it is disclosed by the text. Therefore, your students must learn how to revise their images if they encounter information that requires them to do so.

Sensory Imaging—Sensory imaging employs other senses besides sight, and is closely related to visual imaging. It too has been shown to be crucial to the construction of meaning during reading. This is because the more senses that are employed in a task, the more neural pathways are built, resulting in more avenues to access information. You have experienced sensory imaging when you could almost smell the smoke of a forest fire, taste the sizzling bacon, or as you laughed along with a character as you read. Sensory imaging connects the reader personally and intimately to the text and breathes life into words.

Since visualization is a challenging skill for one out of every five students to develop, begin with simple fictional passages to scaffold their attempts and promote success. After your students have experienced success with visualization and sensory imaging in literature, they are ready to employ these techniques in nonfiction text.

Visualization has a special significance in nonfiction text. The technical presentation of ideas in nonfiction text coupled with new terms and concepts often overwhelm and discourage students. Using visualization can help students move beyond these barriers. As an added benefit, people who create mental images display better long-term retention of factual material.

Clearly, there are important reasons to teach visualization and sensory imaging skills to students. But perhaps the most compelling reason is this: visualizing demands active involvement, turning passive students into active constructors of meaning.

Teaching Visualization Skills *(cont.)*

Doing Think-Alouds—It is essential for you to introduce visualization by doing think-alouds to describe your own visualization of text. To do this, read aloud the first one or two lines of a passage and describe what images come to your mind. Be sure to include details that were not stated in the text, such as the house has two stories and green shutters. Then, read the next two lines, and explain how you add to or modify your image based on the new information provided by the text. When you are doing a think-aloud for your class, be sure to do the following:

- Explain how your images help you to better understand the passage.

- Describe details, being sure to include some from your own schema.

- Mention the use of your senses—the more the better.

- Describe your revision of the images as you read further and encounter new information.

Teaching Summarizing

Summarizing informational text is a crucial skill for students to master. It is also one of the most challenging. Summarizing means pulling out only the essential elements of a passage—just the main idea and supporting details. Research has shown that having students put information into their own words causes it to be processed more thoroughly. Thus, summarizing increases both understanding and long-term retention of material. Information can be summarized through such diverse activities as speaking, writing, drawing, or creating a project.

The basic steps of summarizing are as follows:

- Look for the paragraph's main idea sentence; if there is none, create one.

- Find the supporting details, being certain to group all related terms or ideas.

- Record information that is repeated or restated only once.

- Put the summary together into an organized format.

Scaffolding is of critical importance. Your students will need a lot of modeling, guided practice, and small-group or partner practice before attempting to summarize independently. All strategies should be done as a whole group and then with a partner several times before letting the students practice them on their own. Encourage the greatest transfer of knowledge by modeling each strategy's use in multiple content areas.

Teaching Vocabulary

Students may see a word in print that they have never read or heard before. As a result, students need direct instruction in vocabulary to make real progress toward becoming readers who can independently access expository text. Teaching the vocabulary that occurs in a text significantly improves comprehension. Because students encounter vocabulary terms in science, social studies, math, and language arts, strategies for decoding and understanding new words must be taught throughout the day.

Students' vocabularies develop in this order: listening, speaking, reading, and writing. This means that a child understands a word when it is spoken to him or her long before he or she uses it in speech. The child will also understand the word when reading it before attempting to use it in his or her own writing. Each time a child comes across the same word, his or her understanding of that word deepens. Research has shown that vocabulary instruction has the most positive effect on reading comprehension when students encounter the words multiple times. That is why the best vocabulary instruction requires students to use new words in writing and speaking as well as in reading.

Teaching vocabulary can be both effective and fun, especially if you engage the students' multiple modalities (listening, speaking, reading, and writing). In addition, instruction that uses all four modalities is most apt to reach every learner.

The more experience a child has with language, the stronger his or her vocabulary base. Therefore, the majority of vocabulary activities should be done as whole-group or small-group instruction. In this way, children with a limited vocabulary can learn from their peers' knowledge bases and will find vocabulary activities less frustrating. Remember, too, that a picture is worth a thousand words. Whenever possible, provide pictures of new vocabulary words.

Selecting Vocabulary Words to Study

Many teachers feel overwhelmed when teaching vocabulary because they realize that it is impossible to thoroughly cover all the words students may not know. Do not attempt to study every unknown word. Instead, choose the words from each selection wisely. Following these guidelines in order will result in an educationally sound vocabulary list:

- Choose words that are critical to the article's meaning.
- Choose conceptually difficult words.
- Choose words with the greatest utility value—those that you anticipate the children will see more often (e.g., choose *horrified* rather than *appalled*).

These suggestions are given for teaching nonfiction material in general. Do not select and preteach vocabulary from these practice passages. You want to simulate real test conditions in which the children would have no prior knowledge of any of the material in any of the passages.

Teaching Vocabulary *(cont.)*

Elements of Effective Vocabulary Instruction

Vocabulary instruction is only effective if students permanently add the concepts to their knowledge bases. Research has shown that the most effective vocabulary program includes contextual, structural, and classification strategies. You can do this by making certain that your vocabulary instruction includes the following elements:

- using context clues

- knowing the meaning of affixes (prefixes, suffixes) and roots

- introducing new words as synonyms and antonyms of known words

Using Context Clues

Learning vocabulary in context is important for two reasons. First, it allows students to become active in determining word meanings; and second, it transfers into their lives by offering them a way to figure out unknown words in their independent reading. If you teach your students how to use context clues, you may eventually be able to omit preteaching any vocabulary that is defined in context (so long as the text is written at your students' independent levels).

There are five basic kinds of context clues.

- **Definition**—The definition is given elsewhere in the sentence or paragraph.

  Example: The ragged, *tattered* dress hung from her shoulders.

- **Synonym**—A synonym or synonymous phrase is immediately used in the sentence.

  Example: Although she was overweight, her *obesity* never bothered her until she went to middle school.

- **Contrast**—The meaning may be implied through contrast to a known word or concept. Be alert to these words that signal contrast: *although*, *but*, *however*, and *even though*.

  Example: Although Adesha had always been *prompt*, today he was 20 minutes late.

- **Summary**—The meaning is summed up by a list of attributes.

  Example: Tundra, desert, grassland, and rain forest are four of Earth's *biomes*.

- **Mood**—The meaning of the word can sometimes be grasped from the mood of the larger context in which it appears. The most difficult situation is when the meaning must be inferred with few other clues.

  Example: Her *shrill* voice was actually making my ears hurt.

Teaching Vocabulary (cont.)

Building Vocabulary

Your general approach to building vocabulary should include the following:

Brainstorming—Students brainstorm a list of words associated with a familiar word, sharing everyone's knowledge and thoroughly discussing unfamiliar words.

Semantic mapping—Students sort the brainstormed words into categories, often creating a visual organization tool—such as a graphic organizer or word web—to depict the relationships.

Feature analysis—Students are provided with the key features of the text and a list of terms in a chart, such as a semantic matrix or Venn diagram. Have the students identify the similarities and differences between the items.

Synonyms and antonyms—Introduce both synonyms and antonyms for the words to provide a structure for meaning and substantially and rapidly increase your students' vocabularies.

Analogies—Analogies are similar to synonyms but require higher-level thinking. The goal is to help students identify the relationship between words. Analogies appear on standardized tests in the upper elementary grades.

> **Example:** Bark is to tree as skin is to <u>human</u>.

Word affixes—Studying common prefixes and suffixes helps students deduce new words, especially in context. Teach students to ask, "Does this look like any other word I know? Can I find any word parts I know? Can I figure out the meaning based on its context?"

Important Affixes for Primary Grades

Prefix	Meaning	Example	Suffix	Meaning	Example
un	not	unusual	**-s or -es**	more than one	cars; tomatoes
re	again	redo	**-ed**	did an action	moved
in, im	not	impassable	**-ing**	doing an action	buying
dis	opposite	disassemble	**-ly**	like, very	usually
non	not	nonathletic	**-er**	a person who	farmer
over	too much	overcook	**-ful**	full of	respectful
mis	bad	misrepresent	**-or**	a person who	creator
pre	before	prearrange	**-less**	without	harmless
de	opposite	decompose	**-er**	more	calmer
under	less	underachieve	**-est**	most	happiest

Correlation to Standards

The No Child Left Behind (NCLB) legislation mandates that all states adopt academic standards that identify the skills students will learn in kindergarten through grade 12. While many states had already adopted academic standards prior to NCLB, the legislation set requirements to ensure the standards were detailed and comprehensive.

Standards are designed to focus instruction and guide adoption of curricula. Standards are statements that describe the criteria necessary for students to meet specific academic goals. They define the knowledge, skills, and content students should acquire at each level. Standards are also used to develop standardized tests to evaluate students' academic progress.

In many states today, teachers are required to demonstrate how their lessons meet state standards. State standards are used in the development of Shell Education products, so educators can be assured that they meet the academic requirements of each state.

How to Find Your State Correlations

Shell Education is committed to producing educational materials that are research and standards based. In this effort, all products are correlated to the academic standards of the 50 states, the District of Columbia, and the Department of Defense Dependent Schools. A correlation report customized for your state can be printed directly from the following website: **http://www.shelleducation.com**. If you require assistance in printing correlation reports, please contact Customer Service at 1-877-777-3450.

McREL Compendium

Shell Education uses the Mid-continent Research for Education and Learning (McREL) Compendium to create standards correlations. Each year, McREL analyzes state standards and revises the compendium. By following this procedure, they are able to produce a general compilation of national standards.

Each reading comprehension strategy assessed in this book is based on one or more McREL content standards. The chart shows the McREL standards that correlate to each lesson used in the book. For a state-specific correlation, visit the Shell Education website at **http://www.shelleducation.com**.

Language Arts Standards

Standard 1 **Uses the general skills and strategies of the writing process**

    1.2   Uses strategies to draft and revise written work.

Standard 5 **Uses the general skills and strategies of the reading process.**

    5.1   Uses mental images based on pictures and print to aid in comprehension of text.

    5.2   Uses meaning clues to aid comprehension.

Standard 7 **Uses reading skills and strategies to understand and interpret a variety of informational texts**.

    7.1   Uses reading skills and strategies to understand a variety of informational texts.

    7.2   Understands the main idea and supporting details of simple expository information.

    7.3   Summarizes information found in texts.

    7.4   Relates new information to prior knowledge and experiences.

It's a Sea Monster

Pharagraphy

1   Scientists from the University of Oslo in Norway have made a big splash. They found the skeleton of a reptile that is 150 million years old. The scientists think that no one knew about this kind of sea creature before.

2   The sea monster was 33 feet long. It had teeth the size of bananas. It had backbones as wide as dinner plates. The scientists also found 27 other fossils along with the creature. They were all found in the Arctic Ocean.

3   The skeleton will help scientists identify similar bones found in Britain, Germany, and Russia. The team plans to go back to the place where it found the skeleton. The scientists hope they will find even more bones there.

It's a Sea Monster (cont.)

Directions: Answer these questions. You may look at the article.

1. What do scientists call this creature?

    a. They call it a dinosaur.
    b. They call it a whale.
    c. They call it a sea monster.

2. Where do these scientists work?

    a. They work in Germany.
    b. They work in Norway.
    c. They work in Britain.

3. How big was the creature? Describe <u>two</u> of its features.

    It was 33 feet long.
    It had teeth the size of bananas.

4. Why is this an important discovery?

    The scientists think that no one
    knew about this kind of sea creature
    before.

5. Do you think this creature was a meat eater? Why or why not?

    Yes, because it is huge creature it can
    eat everything in the sea.

6. Where did researchers find these bones? Where else have similar bones been found?

    They founde in the Arctic
    ocean!/ in Britain, Germany and Russia.

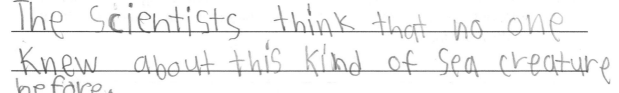

7. How might this discovery help scientists identify similar bones found in other places?

    The team Plans to go back to
    the Place where it found the skeleton.

Name _____

It's a Sea Monster (cont.)

Directions: Look at the picture. Answer the questions.

1. Scientists think this is what the sea monster they found might have looked like. What animal of the sea do you think would have been the sea monster's fiercest enemy? Why do you think that?

   I think the Shark becuse ther fighting becuse the Shark is eating

2. For thousands of years, sailors have told tales of sea serpents, but no one believed their stories. With the recent findings of sea monster fossils, now scientists are wondering if some of the stories were true. What do you think? What do you think sailors really saw during their journeys in the sea?

   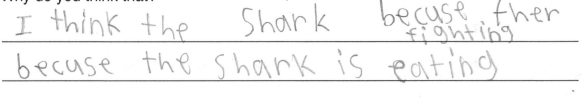

   Yes becuse the Sharks were following the boat behind

Helen Keller

1   Helen Keller was born in 1880 in Tuscumbia, Alabama. When she was a baby, an illness left her blind and deaf. It seemed she would never understand the world around her. But she became a shining example to other people with disabilities.

2   When Helen was six, her parents hired a special teacher, Anne Sullivan. She taught Helen to connect hand signs with word meanings. Helen soon learned to communicate with sign language and Braille. Braille is a language of raised dots that blind people read with their fingers. Helen even learned to speak.

3   Keller later worked to help blind people around the world. A blind person, she said, "has a mind that can be educated, a hand that can be trained."

illness: sickness
deaf: you can't hear
example: something that tells you what something is
disabilities: something someone is born with or sick that can slow down someones learning.
example: rolemodel

Tuscumbia
Alabama
example
disabilities
Sulivan
Braile
educated
trained:

Helen Keller *(cont.)*

Directions: Answer these questions. You may look at the article.

1. How did Helen Keller become blind and deaf?

    a. She was born that way.

    b. An illness left her that way.

    c. An accident left her that way.

2. How old was Helen when her parents hired her teacher?

    a. She was a baby.

    b. She was a teenager.

    c. She was six years old.

3. What are two things that Anne Sullivan taught Helen that helped her to communicate?

    She taught sign language and Braille.

4. What did Helen do later in life to help others?

    Helen helped Blind People around the world.

5. Close your eyes and imagine for a moment that you are blind and deaf. List three sounds that you think you would most miss hearing. Now list three things that you would most miss seeing.

    ① mom's voice   ① family
    ② brothers voice ② tv Bible
    ③ music

6. Imagine how sensitive your other senses would become if you could not see or hear. List three things that you might become better at doing.

    taste
    speake
    smell

#50242—*Comprehension and Critical Thinking*   © *Shell Education*

Helen Keller (cont.)

Directions: Look at this chart. Answer the questions.

Using Your Senses

Which senses help you identify the items below?	Sight	Hearing	Touch	Smell	Taste
Ice Cream	X				X
Dog	X	X	X	X	
Guitar	X	X	X		
Rose	X		X	X	
Cookies	X		X	X	X

1. Do you think one more sense could help you identify an ice cream cone? Explain which sense that is and how that sense might help you.

   touch. Because I feels cold and it melts, sticky and smooth.

2. Which sense do you think it would be hardest to live without? Which one do you think would be the easiest to live without? Why?

   ① Hearing!
   ② Smell. Because bad smell can't go in my nose.
   =I don't have to smell bad things.

3. Think of something that you would be able to identify immediately with your other senses if you were deaf and blind. What is it? Why would you be able to tell what it was so quickly?

   Touch. Because to touch you can tell what an object is by it's shape, texture, and size.

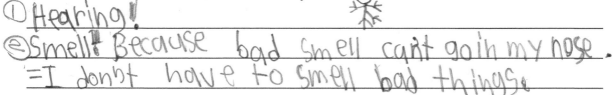

A Discovery Worth Chirping About

A sharp-eyed bird-watcher in India has made a rare discovery. Ramana Athreya spotted a brand-new species, or kind of bird. He found the small, colorful bird in a forest in India.

In May 2006, Athreya was able to study the bird up close. He took pictures and made careful notes. He also collected feathers. Athreya's research helped show scientists that the bird was a new species. This is the first new type of bird found in India in more than 50 years.

Athreya named the bird after a nearby tribe called the *Buguns*. Scientists know of only 14 of the birds in the area. Athreya and a team of researchers plan to search for more. "It makes me think of all the other species—butterflies, reptiles, insects, plants—waiting to be discovered!" Athreya said.

A Discovery Worth Chirping About (cont.)

Directions: Answer these questions. You may look at the article.

1. Why was this discovery so important?
   a. It identified a new species of butterfly.
   b. It identified a bird that scientists thought was extinct.
   c. It identified a new species of bird.

2. What name was chosen for the new species?
   a. Athreya
   b. Buguns
   c. Ramana

3. What type of research did Athreya do to study the bird?

   Athreyae was able to study the bird up close.

4. What do you think are two important things bird-watchers look for?

   He took pictures and made careful notes. and He also colleted feathers.

5. How do you think researchers count the number of birds in an area? How would they be able to tell that they were not seeing the same bird again and again?

   tible called the Bugnus. scientists know of ofny 14 of the birds

6. What do you imagine this new bird looks like? On the back of this paper, draw a picture of it, based on the clues in the passage.

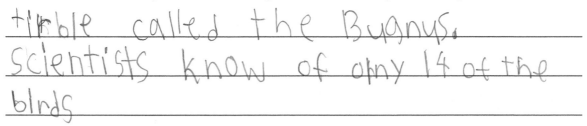

A Discovery Worth Chirping About (cont.)

Directions: Look at the picture. Answer the questions.

1. Imagine you are a bird-watcher. What do you think you can figure out about what these birds are doing and the way they live? Can you predict what will happen next?

   tha birds is a holding a worm
   and the bird will give it to
   the baby bird.

2. Why do you think so many people enjoy bird-watching?

   they are cute and their in a
   nest in a tree too.

#50242—*Comprehension and Critical Thinking*   © *Shell Education*

Remembering Rosa Parks

In 1955, Rosa Parks made history by breaking the law. Her crime? Sitting where she wanted on a public bus in Montgomery, Alabama. That would not be a big deal today. But back then, laws in some states required separate seating for black people and white people. Parks was a black woman. She was arrested for not giving her seat to a white man.

After Parks' arrest, many African-Americans refused to ride buses in Montgomery. They refused for 381 days. In 1956, the United States Supreme Court did away with separate seating on buses. In 1964, the Civil Rights Act made racial discrimination in public places against the law.

Parks died at the age of 92. Many think of her as the mother of the civil rights movement.

Remembering Rosa Parks (cont.)

Directions: Answer these questions. You may look at the article.

1. What did Rosa Parks do in 1955 that made history?
   a. She refused to get off a bus.
   b. She refused to give her bus seat to a white man.
   c. She refused to get on a bus just for black people.

2. What did black people in Montgomery do to protest Parks' arrest?
   a. They stopped riding public buses.
   b. They stopped giving up their bus seats.
   c. They stopped driving buses.

3. How do you think it felt for black people to be forced to only sit on certain parts of the bus?

   They will feel mad or they
   will feel sad.

   _____

4. How long did it take after Parks' arrest for the United States Supreme Court to make it against the law to have separate seating for blacks and whites?

   They refused for 381 days.

5. What did the Civil Rights Act do?

   Civil Right Act made racial
   discrimination in Pyblelid Plases
   against the law.

6. Can you think of a time when you felt discriminated against because you were a kid? If yes, describe the experience and what it felt like. If no, describe a time when you saw someone else being discriminated against.

   Yes when I was in 1st grade
   I felt mad when other
   call me bad words.

1912
XXXXX
- 1955
(67)

Remembering Rosa Parks (cont.)

Directions: Look at the time line. Answer the questions.

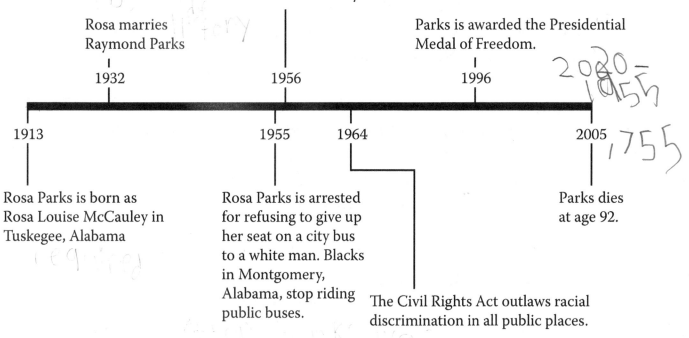

U.S. Supreme Court rules that African Americans
cannot be forced to sit only in certain areas on buses.

Rosa marries
Raymond Parks

Parks is awarded the Presidential
Medal of Freedom.

2020 -
1955
1932   1956   1996

1755

1913   1955   1964   2005

Rosa Parks is born as
Rosa Louise McCauley in
Tuskegee, Alabama

Rosa Parks is arrested
for refusing to give up
her seat on a city bus
to a white man. Blacks
in Montgomery,
Alabama, stop riding
public buses.

The Civil Rights Act outlaws racial
discrimination in all public places.

Parks dies
at age 92.

1. How many years ago did Parks challenge the seating laws on buses?

   It was in 1955.

2. How many years later was she honored by the president?

   It will be 67 years.

3. Parks received many tributes and honors during her life. What do you think would be
   a good way for each of us to honor Rosa Parks' memory?

   we are gonna honer Rosa Parks.

   _____

Saving the Great Apes

Gorillas, chimpanzees, bonobos, and orangutans are called the great apes. These fascinating creatures are smart and social. They can act a lot like humans! But sadly, humans haven't treated them well. They are dying out in their homelands in central Africa and Southeast Asia. Scientists worry that the apes could disappear forever.

But there is now some good news for great apes. Recently, 23 nations signed a pact to work harder to protect them. Most of the nations that signed the agreement are in Africa and Asia, where great apes still live in the wild. The United States and other wealthy nations have promised to help pay for programs to keep the apes safe.

James Deutsch of the Wildlife Conservation Society said that getting countries to agree to act is a big step. But these nations have many problems. Their people need food and jobs. "The great apes live in some of the poorest countries," says Deutsch. "They will need help and money."

It will be a challenge to save the great apes. But the nations involved have agreed that our world would be a poorer place without these amazing animals.

Saving the Great Apes (cont.)

Directions: Answer these questions. You may look at the article.

1. Where do the great apes live?
   a. Asia and North America
   b. Africa and Asia
   c. South America and Africa

2. What is the good news for the great apes?
   a. They are no longer in danger.
   b. The countries where they live are now wealthy.
   c. Nations are now working together to protect them.

3. What four kinds of animals are called the *great apes*?

   gorillas, chimpanzees, bonobos, orangutans

4. What are some of the problems in the countries where these apes live?

   Their people need food and jobs.

5. With the problems facing the people of these countries, why is it important to save the apes?

   Our world wold be a poorere place without these amazing animals.

6. Who is James Deutsch?

   James Detsch of the widelife conservation a member

7. Have you ever seen great apes at the zoo or on TV and thought about how humanlike they appear? What is it about them that most reminds you of a human?

   Yes becuse it's a wild animal the acting is good

Saving the Great Apes (cont.)

Directions: Look at the pictures and read the descriptions. Answer these questions.

Orangutan	Gorilla
• My body is covered with long hair.	• I am the largest of the great apes.
• I can have orange, brown, or red hair.	• I have a large chest and thick arms.
• I have hook-shaped hands and feet.	• I am covered in black or gray hair.
• My long arms help me climb.	• I may be big, but I am gentle.
• I like to eat fruit, leaves, and bark.	• I eat leaves, stems, and fruits.
• I spend most of my life in trees.	• I live mostly on the ground.

1. What is one similarity between the orangutan and the gorilla?

   they eat fruits and leaves.

   _____

2. What is one difference between the orangutan and the gorilla?

   orangutan has orange brown red hair
   Gorilla has black or gray hair

3. How do you think the arms of the orangutan help it live in trees?

   ith's long arms help orangutan
   climb.

The Art of Storytelling

Before television came to Japan, children were entertained by *kamishibai*. Kamishibai is paper theater. Each day, the kamishibai man rode his bicycle into town and smacked two wooden blocks together. *Clack! Clack!* The children rushed outside. As the kamishibai man told his tales, he held up cards. On the cards were scenes he had painted that brought his stories to life.

Allen Say is an author and illustrator. He grew up in Japan. He has written and illustrated a new book called *Kamishibai Man*. In it, Say's watercolor paintings tell the story of his favorite childhood memory.

"The sound of those clappers!" Say remembered, "I waited for it all afternoon."

The Art of Storytelling (cont.)

Directions: Answer these questions. You may look at the article.

1. What is *kamishibai*?

   a. It is a kind of Japanese food.

   b. It is a card game.

   (c.) It is paper theater.

2. How did the kamishibai man let children know he arrived?

   a. He called to them in the street.

   b. He made loud sounds using wooden blocks.

   c. He put flyers up around town.

3. What did Allen Say do?

   Axllen Say is an author and illustaned.

4. What kind of artwork does he do?

   He grew up JaPanman,

5. How did he know about the kamishibai man?

   in its says watercolon Painting tell the story

6. Do you think life is better or worse with television? Explain your answer.

   worse becuse it will hurt Yoan eyes.

7. What kinds of things do you think children did before they had television and electronics? How do you think your life would be different if you did not have any of those things?

   I think they wachted tv for a long time

The Art of Storytelling (cont.)

Directions: Look at the kamishibai cards. Respond to the prompt below.

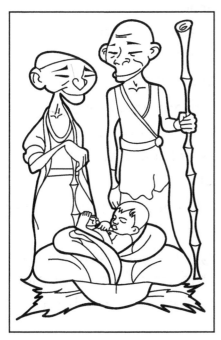

Imagine you are the kamishibai man telling a story to children. Write a short story based on these pictures. Give your story a beginning, middle, and end.

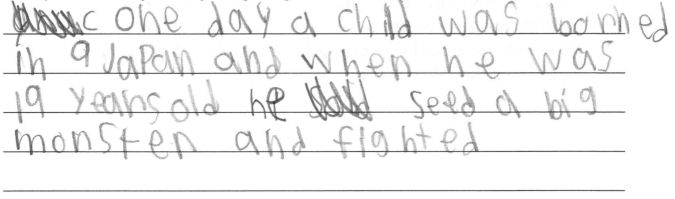

one day a child was borned in a Japan and when he was 19 years old he seed a big monster and fighted

Earth Smart

Spring has sprung at Goodwillie Environmental School in Ada, Michigan. There are 96 fifth- and sixth-graders who go there. They call the outdoors their living classroom. The students will learn about wildflowers and spend an evening tracking frogs.

Goodwillie is a green school. Green schools use less energy than regular schools. Solar panels capture the sun's power to heat the school in winter. The walls and floors are made with material that has been recycled from used objects.

The teachers and students at Goodwillie believe that knowing about nature helps them love and respect it. They spend part of nearly every day outside, even during Michigan's cold winter. Kids might collect sap from a tree, visit the school pond, or pick up trash along the road. They take turns cleaning the school's chicken coop.

Students also study the life cycles of plants and animals. They draw sketches of the things they see outdoors. They try to keep track of changes from season to season. Clara Cullen says that spending time outside has opened her eyes. "It's amazing how much is out there," she says.

Earth Smart *(cont.)*

Directions: Answer these questions. You may look at the article.

1. What is a green school?

   a. It is a school that only uses recycled materials.

   b. It is a school that uses less energy than regular schools.

   c. It is a school that plants all its own food.

2. How does Goodwillie conserve energy?

   a. Most classes are taught outside.

   b. It doesn't use any fuel.

   c. Solar panels capture the sun's heat to keep the school warm.

3. List four things that Goodwillie students do that put them in touch with nature.

   _____

   _____

4. What are recycled materials used for at the school?

   _____

5. What is something that you learned in school that has taught you to appreciate nature?

   _____

   _____

6. What makes your school different from Goodwillie? Explain.

   _____

   _____

7. If you had the chance to go to a school like this, would you? Why or why not?

   _____

   _____

   _____

Earth Smart *(cont.)*

Directions: Read the chart. Answer the questions.

Get Green

Here is how to save energy and help the environment:

Light Savers	Turn off the lights in empty rooms. This bright idea can bring big savings on energy costs.
Reuse, Recycle	Reusing paper, cans, bottles, and batteries cuts down on costs and waste. Use both sides of notebook paper. Carry a lunch box instead of a paper bag. Recycle whatever you cannot reuse.
Don't Be a Drip	Leaky faucets can waste large amounts of water over time. Even a small stream adds up. Report any drips you see to someone who can fix them.

1. Describe a room in your house where a light or appliance is usually on, but does not have to be. How will you remember to turn it off when it is not being used?

   _____

   _____

   _____

2. Write about a way you can reuse some of your school supplies or something at home that you would otherwise throw away.

   _____

   _____

   _____

3. Write about a way you can use less water at home. Do you think this will be hard?

   _____

   _____

   _____

A True Look at Washington

Researchers are changing the way Americans look at George Washington. The staff at Mount Vernon, Washington's home in Virginia, set out to make models that truly look like the father of our country. They wanted to show how he looked at 19 as a young man. They also wanted to show how he looked at 45 as a military leader, and at 57 as the first United States President.

A team of artists in New York City made the models. They worked with information that scientists gathered.

Washington rarely posed for paintings. That is why many portraits don't look like him. Scientist Jeffrey Schwartz and a group of researchers studied Washington's hair samples, dentures, eyeglasses, and clothing.

When Washington was 53, a French sculptor measured his body. He then made a mask of his face. The mask became the best clue of all. It was used to make a computer model of Washington. "Certain bony places on his forehead and cheeks would be the same throughout his life," Schwartz said.

A True Look at Washington (cont.)

Directions: Answer these questions. You may look at the article.

1. Where is George Washington's home?

   a. Washington, D.C.

   b. New York City

   c. Mount Vernon, Virginia

2. Why was it so hard to figure out what Washington really looked like?

   a. Most pictures of him have been lost.

   b. He didn't often pose for paintings.

   c. He changed his physical appearance often.

3. What four items of Washington's did scientists study to try to figure out what he really looked like?

   _____

   _____

4. What three ages of Washington's life do researchers want to show with models? Why do you think they chose those ages?

   _____

   _____

5. Why do you think this was an important project to the researchers, scientists, and artists involved?

   _____

   _____

6. Do you think that you get a better sense of who a historical figure really was if you are able to see an exact replica of what he or she looked like? Why or why not?

   _____

   _____

   _____

A True Look at Washington *(cont.)*

Directions: Look at the three models of George Washington. Answer the questions.

Three Stages of Washington's Life

1. Which model do you think shows Washington when he was 19 years old? How can you tell?

   _____

2. What do you think he is doing in the model in which his hand is on the Bible?

   _____

   _____

3. How do you think it would feel to have to dress in such formal clothing? Do you think you would have liked living in the 1700s?

   _____

   _____

More Room to Roam

Some elephants at the Pittsburgh Zoo may be packing up their trunks for a big move. The zoo just bought a large new home for elephants. The area includes forests, ponds, and rolling fields.

The zoo plans to turn the land into a conservation center for African elephants. Zoo officials will set up a breeding program. They hope that the elephant population will grow from just six to 20.

Elephants are seriously threatened. There are only between 300,000 and 600,000 African elephants left in the wild. About one million lived in the wild 20 years ago.

The Pittsburgh Zoo is in Pennsylvania. It is the only large United States city zoo to create a conservation center for elephants. Zoo President Barbara Baker hopes these efforts will help remind people that these creatures need our protection. She says that if nothing is done, United States zoos will see their numbers dwindle.

In ten years, Baker would like to see the center bustling with baby elephants and their mothers. "Elephants create such excitement and wonder about wildlife," she said. "I would hate to lose that."

More Room to Roam *(cont.)*

Directions: Answer these questions. You may look at the article.

1. In what state is the Pittsburgh Zoo located?

    a. California

    b. Pennsylvania

    c. New York

2. About how many African elephants are left in the wild today?

    a. between 300,000 and 600,000

    b. one million

    c. 20

3. Why do zoo officials want to open a conservation center?

    _____

    _____

4. How many elephants does the zoo hope to have after it sets up a breeding program? How many more is that than it has now?

    _____

    _____

5. What are some of the reasons you think the elephants' population might be threatened?

    _____

    _____

6. Do you think elephants would be happier at a conservation center or at a zoo? Why?

    _____

    _____

7. Zoo officials worry that unless something is done to help the elephants, United States zoos will see their numbers dwindle. What do you think *dwindle* means?

    _____

More Room to Roam (cont.)

Directions: Look at the graph. Answer the questions.

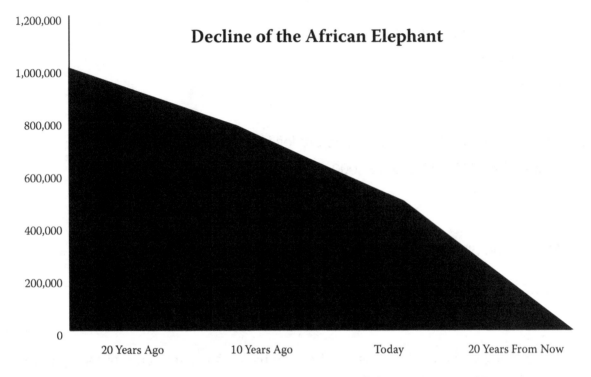

1. About how many African elephants were in the wild 20 years ago?

   _____

2. How many elephants do researchers estimate there are today?

   _____

3. If nothing is done to protect the elephants, what does the chart indicate might happen 20 years from now?

   _____

4. If many zoos build conservation centers, how many elephants do you predict there might be in 20 years? What is one thing you could do to help?

   _____

   _____

Walk Through History

Have you ever wondered what it would be like to stand in the shoes of people who fought for equality? At the International Civil Rights Walk of Fame, visitors can come close. The walk opened recently in Atlanta, Georgia.

The shoe prints of 17 civil rights leaders are carved into sections of the walk. The leaders fought for the equal treatment of African-Americans. The walk includes the shoe prints of Rosa Parks and former presidents Jimmy Carter and Lyndon Johnson.

The walk was Xernona Clayton's idea. She plans to add 600 more shoe prints. "We have to educate (kids) to the contribution that civil rights warriors have made to this country," says Clayton.

Walk Through History *(cont.)*

Directions: Answer these questions. You may look at the article.

1. Who is honored at this Walk of Fame?

   a. government leaders

   b. movie stars

   c. civil rights leaders

2. How does the Walk of Fame honor the leaders?

   a. by carving their shoe prints into the walk

   b. by giving them stars on the walk

   c. by carving their initials into the walk

3. Why did Xernona Clayton take on this project?

   _____

   _____

4. Where is the walk located?

   _____

5. What do you think it means that it is the International Walk of Fame?

   _____

6. How many civil rights leaders were honored when the walk opened? How many more does Clayton plan to honor?

   _____

7. How do you think the people being honored and their families must feel about being inducted into the Walk of Fame? Describe how you would feel if you were being honored.

   _____

   _____

Walk Through History (cont.)

Directions: Look at the chart. Answer the questions.

Civil Rights Walk of Fame Honorees

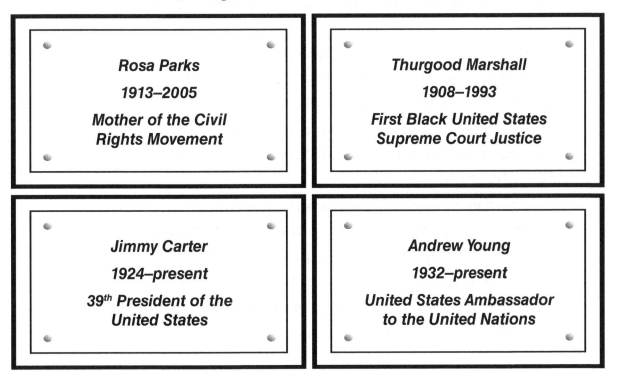

Rosa Parks

1913–2005

Mother of the Civil Rights Movement

Thurgood Marshall

1908–1993

First Black United States Supreme Court Justice

Jimmy Carter

1924–present

39th President of the United States

Andrew Young

1932–present

United States Ambassador to the United Nations

1. How many of these leaders were alive when the chart above was created?

   _____

2. Which of these leaders served in the United Nations? Which one served on the United States' highest court?

   _____

   _____

3. Do you think that every one of the honorees in the Civil Rights Walk of Fame is an African-American? Explain why you think that it would or would not matter.

   _____

   _____

The Flight That Changed the World

The morning of December 17, 1903 was cold and windy in Kitty Hawk, North Carolina. But two brothers headed to the beach anyway.

Orville and Wilbur Wright hoped to get their invention off the ground. It was an engine-powered plane called the *Flyer*. They had built it in their bike shop in Dayton, Ohio.

At 10:35 A.M., Orville flew the plane first. Wilbur took a turn at flying, too. The brothers made history by taking the first airplane flight in the world.

As kids, Orville and Wilbur played with kites and a flying toy. They worked to solve the mystery of flight as they grew.

Studying birds gave them an idea. The brothers built wings to help steer and balance the plane. They also made propellers that worked like birds' wings. Those propellers pushed the plane—and the Wrights—into history.

The Flight That Changed the World (cont.)

Directions: Answer these questions. You may look at the article.

1. What city were the Wright brothers in when they took their first flight?

   a. Columbia, Sorth Carolina
   b. Kitty Hawk, North Carolina
   c. Dayton, Ohio

2. When did the Wright brothers take their first flight?

   a. December 17, 1903
   b. December 17, 1913
   c. November 17, 1903

3. What kind of shop did they build their plane in?

   _____

4. What were the Wright brothers' favorite toys as children? What do the toys have in common? What do some of your favorite toys say about your interests?

   _____

   _____

5. What two parts of the plane did the Wright brothers get ideas about by studying birds?

   _____

   _____

6. The Wright brothers failed with their flying experiments many times before they succeeded. Describe a time when you felt like giving up, but you kept trying and finally succeeded. How did it feel to achieve your goal? Use the back of this paper if more space is needed.

   _____

   _____

   _____

The Flight That Changed the World (cont.)

Directions: Look at the pictures. Answer the questions.

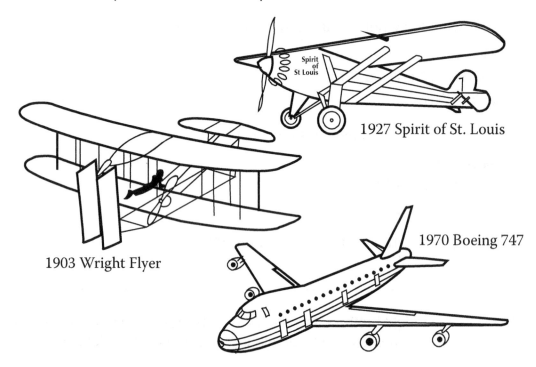

1927 Spirit of St. Louis

1903 Wright Flyer

1970 Boeing 747

1. List two things that all these aircraft have in common. List two things that are different about the Boeing 747.

   _____

   _____

   _____

2. Why do you think engineers keep inventing different kinds of aircraft?

   _____

   _____

3. If you were going on a trip, in which type of plane do you think you would most likely fly?

   _____

   _____

Kids Tune in Too Much

Are young kids glued to their TVs too much of the day? To find out, a family health group asked questions of more than 1,000 parents. The study found that small children spend as much time in front of video screens as they spend outdoors.

Kids age six and under spend about two hours a day outside. They also spend two hours watching TV, using a computer, or playing video games.

The study found that kids who watch a lot of TV are more likely to have problems reading. Kids age six and under spend less than 40 minutes a day reading or being read to.

Even toddlers tune in too much. About four out of 10 kids under age two watch TV every day. Peggy Charren is an expert on children's television. "This seems like too much for little kids to be watching," she says.

Kids Tune in Too Much (cont.)

Directions: Answer these questions. You may look at the article.

1. About how many hours a day do kids six and under spend outside?

    a. one hour

    b. six hours

    c. two hours

2. How much time do kids six and under usually spend reading or being read to everyday?

    a. two hours

    b. 40 minutes

    c. four hours

3. Of the time young kids spend in front of a screen, do you think most of it is TV, computers, or video games?

    _____

4. Peggy Charren says it seems that young kids are spending too much time watching TV. Do you agree or disagree? Explain your answer.

    _____

    _____

5. What would happen if you came home one day and your parents had gotten rid of every TV in your house? What would you do? List three activities you would plan for a week with no TV.

    _____

    _____

    _____

6. Do your parents have a limit on how much TV you watch every day? Do you think they should? Why or why not?

    _____

    _____

Kids Tune in Too Much *(cont.)*

Directions: Look at the picture. Answer the questions.

1. Where are these kids? What are they doing?

   _____

   _____

   _____

2. How much time every day do you do what these kids are doing? Do you think that is enough?

   _____

   _____

3. What is your favorite outside activity? Would you rather be outside playing or watching TV?

   _____

   _____

The Big Prize for Peace

Shirin Ebadi works to protect the rights of the people in Iran. Her work earned her the 2003 Nobel Peace Prize.

"This prize doesn't belong to me only," Ebadi said. "It belongs to all people who work for human rights and democracy in Iran."

The Peace Prize is one of the biggest honors in the world. It is given each year to the world's top peacemaker. Ebadi, 56, is the first person from Iran and the first Muslim woman to receive it.

Ebadi's mother, Mino, 79, is very proud of her daughter. When Mino learned about her daughter's award, she said that she cried all day. "I always wanted to become just like Shirin became," she said.

The Big Prize for Peace (cont.)

Directions: Answer these questions. You may look at the article.

1. What is the name of the prize that Shirin Ebadi won?

   a. She won the Pulitzer Prize.

   b. She won the Nobel Peace Prize.

   c. She won the Iranian Peace Prize.

2. Why did she win it?

   a. She won it for her work bringing countries in the Middle East together.

   b. She won it for her work on behalf of women's rights.

   c. She won it for her work protecting the rights of Iranians.

3. What is the Nobel Peace Prize? Who is chosen to receive it?

   _____

   _____

4. Why do you think Ebadi's mother cried when she found out that her daughter was getting the award?

   _____

   _____

5. What do you think she meant when she said she "always wanted to become just like Shirin became?"

   _____

   _____

6. How do you think it would feel to receive an award given to one of the world's top peacemakers? Explain your answer.

   _____

   _____

The Big Prize for Peace (cont.)

Directions: Look at the medals. Answer the questions.

| Medal for the Nobel Prize in Literature | Medal for the Nobel Prize in Peace | Medal for the Nobel Prize in Economics |

Medal for the Nobel Prize in Medicine   Medal for the Nobel Prize in Chemistry   Medal for the Nobel Prize in Physics

1. How many different Nobel Prizes are there?

_____

2. Which two prizes are represented by the same medal? Why do you think that is?

_____

_____

3. What do you think the prize in literature is given for? How does the artwork on the medal symbolize literature?

_____

_____

4. How does the artwork on the Peace Prize medal symbolize peace?

_____

_____

Daddy Day Care

In Kenya, a country in Africa, wild savanna baboons live with elephants, antelope, and other animals. Mother baboons keep their babies clean and protect them.

But baboon moms aren't on the job alone. Last month, scientists reported a surprising discovery. Many baboon dads also take care of their babies. Researchers had thought that male baboons didn't even know which babies were theirs.

For three years, scientists studied 75 baboon babies and their fathers. Half the dads helped raise their babies. Male baboons are tough. But according to Joan Silk, they "can be really sweet with infants." Silk is a college teacher who worked on the study. The dads also protected their young in fights more often than they helped other baboon babies.

Male baboons may know their babies by how they look and smell. Silk says baboon dads are a bit like human dads. Says Silk, "It's fun to find out that animals are smarter than you thought!"

Daddy Day Care (cont.)

Directions: Answer these questions. You may look at the article.

1. Where do wild savanna baboons live?

   a. Asia

   b. Kenya

   c. South America

2. How many baboons did the scientists study?

   a. 100

   b. 20

   c. 75

3. What are two other kinds of animals that wild baboons live with?

   _____

4. What did researchers find out about male baboons? Why were they surprised by their findings?

   _____

   _____

   _____

5. How do male baboons identify their young?

   _____

6. What would happen to the baby baboon if neither the mother or father baboon took care of it?

   _____

   _____

7. Who is Joan Silk? To whom does she compare male baboons?

   _____

   _____

Name _____

Daddy Day Care (cont.)

Directions: Look at the picture. Answer the questions.

1. What do you think this picture shows? What is happening?

   _____

   _____

2. How might a father baboon protect his young?

   _____

   _____

3. Do you think a mother baboon or father baboon would be better at fighting off other animals? Explain your answer.

   _____

   _____

Make Room for the New Kids

Most kids get nervous before the school year starts. Michelle Meyers, 10, was extra worried. "I'm afraid I'm going to get lost!" Michelle said before her first day. She is a new student at W.S. Boardman Elementary in Oceanside, New York.

About one out of seven kids move each year. Like Michelle, most of them end up at a new school. This year, schools may see many more new faces.

David Kerbow studies why kids change schools. He and other experts say that a law called the *No Child Left Behind Act* is one reason more kids are changing schools. The law lets parents switch kids to schools where test scores are higher. Kerbow also says that when people are out of work, "families are more likely to move in search of jobs." It is a hard time for workers.

Being new can be tough. Schools like Hopkins Academy in Texas try to make it easier. New students visit their classrooms with their parents before school starts. They tour the building and meet teachers and students. Michelle's visit to Boardman helped make her first day fun. She didn't get lost! "By noon, I knew my way around the whole school," she says. She isn't nervous anymore!

Make Room for the New Kids (cont.)

Directions: Answer these questions. You may look at the article.

1. How old was Michele Meyers when she moved?

   a. She was six years old.

   b. She was 10 years old.

   c. She was 14 years old.

2. What is the name of her new school?

   a. Oceanside Academy

   b. Hopkins Academy

   c. W.S. Boardman Elementary

3. What law lets parents switch kids to schools where test scores are higher? Do you think that is a good thing or not? Explain your answer.

   _____

   _____

4. Did you have a tour of your school before your first day? If so, did it make your first day easier? If not, do you think it would have? Explain your answer.

   _____

   _____

5. How would you feel if you had to switch schools? Describe how you would feel about starting at a new school where you did not know anyone.

   _____

   _____

6. Everyone is nervous or excited on the first day of school. What are some of the things that made you feel less nervous and more comfortable about the first few days or weeks of a new school year?

   _____

   _____

Make Room for the New Kids *(cont.)*

Directions: Look at the picture. Answer the questions.

1. It is the girl's first day at her new school. How do you think she feels?

   _____

   _____

2. If you were a student in that class, how would you treat the new girl on her first day? Would you go up and talk to her? How would you want to be treated if you were the new kid in class?

   _____

   _____

   _____

3. Think of a time you felt like you did not belong. What did you do to handle the situation?

   _____

   _____

Thurgood Marshall

Thurgood Marshall was born in Baltimore, Maryland, in 1908. As a boy, Marshall spent a lot of time at the local courthouse. He liked to watch the trials. He grew up to be one of the most important civil rights lawyers of his time. In 1967, Marshall became the first black person to serve on the United States Supreme Court.

Marshall fought for equality for African-Americans. On May 17, 1954, he won an important victory as a lawyer. The decision was in a case called *Brown versus Board of Education of Topeka*. It made it against the law to have separate public schools for blacks and whites. This ruling helped improve education for black children.

Marshall retired from the Supreme Court in 1991. He died in 1993.

Thurgood Marshall *(cont.)*

Directions: Answer these questions. You may look at the article.

1. How did Marshall become interested in law?

    a. He enjoyed watching trials at the courthouse.

    b. His grandfather was a lawyer.

    c. He read books about the law.

2. What was one of Marshall's most important cases as a lawyer?

    a. It was a case that won equality for women at work.

    b. It was a case that won equality for black college students.

    c. It was a case that won equality for black public schoolchildren.

3. What was the name of that case?

    _____

4. Before he won that case, what was public school like for black and white children?

    _____

5. What do you think school would be like if children of different colors went to different schools? Explain your answer.

    _____

    _____

    _____

6. How did Marshall make history on the United States Supreme Court?

    _____

    _____

7. How many years was it between the time Marshall retired from the court and the time he died?

    _____

Thurgood Marshall (cont.)

Directions: Look at the list. Answer the questions.

Longest-Serving Justices of the United States Supreme Court (Top 10)

Name	Years Served
1. William O. Douglas	1939–1975
2. Stephen Johnson Field	1863–1897
3. John Marshall	1801–1835
4. Hugo Black	1937–1971
5. John Marshall Harlan	1877–1911
6. William J. Brennan	1956–1990
7. William Rehnquist	1972–2005
8. Joseph Story	1812–1845
9. James Moore Wayne	1835–1867
10. John McLean	1830–1861

1. Five of the 10 justices served the same number of years. How many years did those five justices serve?

   _____

2. Which of the justices served most recently?

   _____

3. Which two justices each served in two centuries?

   _____

   _____

The New Kids' Museums

The Children's Museum of Indianapolis is the biggest of its kind. Soon, kids will be able to explore real baby dinosaur fossils in a new exhibit there.

Visitors to the Indiana museum will hear the sounds, smell the smells, and see the plants and rocks that might have surrounded dinosaurs. Then visitors can dig for model fossils. They can paint or sculpt their own dinosaurs in an art studio.

More than 100 children's museums have opened in the United States since 1990. Now there are more than 200! There are 80 more that are getting ready to open.

These museums are not just filled with old objects to look at and read about. At some, kids can play musical instruments. At others, they can build machines or try on clothes from other countries.

Children's museums are more popular than ever. Last year, at least 31 million people came to learn and explore. That is more than three times the number of visitors in 1991.

Many museums also have activities for parents to do with their children. Dovid Lasson, 8, says his parents enjoy visiting Baltimore's Port Discovery Museum in Maryland as much as he does. "They like to make stuff and do activities and see kids having fun," says Dovid. "We all like going together."

The New Kids' Museums (cont.)

Directions: Answer these questions. You may look at the article.

1. About how many children's museums are there in the United States?

   a. 80

   b. 200

   c. 100

2. What will the new exhibit at the Children's Museum of Indianapolis allow?

   a. It will allow visitors to build machines.

   b. It will allow visitors to play musical instruments.

   c. It will allow visitors to dig for dinosaur fossils.

3. How many people visited children's museums last year? About how many people visited in 1991?

   _____

4. Which children's museum does Dovid Lasson visit with his parents?

   _____

5. What are three things the story says you can do at some children's museums?

   _____

   _____

6. Of those three things, which sounds like the most fun to you? Explain why you think that activity would be your favorite.

   _____

   _____

7. Have you ever been to a museum that was just for grown-ups? If so, what was that like? Do we need special museums just for kids? Why or why not?

   _____

   _____

The New Kids' Museums (cont.)

Directions: Look at the picture. Answer the questions.

1. Where do you think these kids are? What are they doing?

   _____

   _____

   _____

2. Which activity looks likes something you would enjoy? Why?

   _____

   _____

3. Pretend you are in charge of a children's museum. Describe a new exhibit that you think would be the most popular activity at your museum. Use many details in your description.

   _____

   _____

   _____

Alien Invasion

The United States is being invaded by aliens. Strange creatures are popping up in ponds and forests. There might even be some in your own backyard!

This tale isn't as creepy as it sounds. The aliens aren't from outer space. They are plants and animals that have come to the United States from other countries. Some species were brought to the United States on purpose. Others, like the Asian long-horned beetle, arrived here by accident.

Recently, northern snakehead fish were found in a pond in Maryland. This fish is from Southeast Asia, where it has predators. United States wildlife officials were worried because the snakehead has no enemies here. What it does have is a huge appetite!

"Predators of this kind have been among our most damaging species," says scientist Daniel Simberloff. This month, officials poisoned the lake where the snakeheads lived. Not all alien species are bad. But scientists want to keep out those that harm native species. Researcher Faith Campbell said, "We have a responsibility to take care of the environment."

Alien Invasion (cont.)

Directions: Answer these questions. You may look at the article.

1. What kind of aliens is this story about?

    a. This story is about aliens from outer space.

    b. It is about animals and plants from other countries.

    c. It is about a snakefish.

2. According to the story, what kind of alien species arrived in the United States by accident?

    a. the Asian long-horned beetle

    b. the purple loosestrife

    c. the fruit fly

3. Why did the snakehead cause a problem? Why did United States wildlife officials poison the lake?

    _____

    _____

4. How do you think alien plants and animals get into the United States?

    _____

5. Do you think people should be allowed to bring plants and animals into the United States from other countries without asking permission from the United States government? Why or why not?

    _____

    _____

6. Do you think it is all right for scientists to try to keep out plants and animals that might harm species that are native to the United States? Why or why not?

    _____

    _____

    _____

Alien Invasion (cont.)

Directions: Look at the map. Answer the questions.

United States Invasion of Long-Horned Beetles

Asian long-horned beetles have been destroying trees in several states in the United States. The dots on the map show where the beetles have been spotted. The stars show where they have infested some areas.

1. What state has the highest number of long-horned beetles? List two other states where the beetles have been spotted.

   _____

   _____

2. Why do you think the beetles seem to be in only a few parts of the country?

   _____

   _____

3. What do you think will happen if the beetles spread all over the country?

   _____

   _____

The New Gym

It's a sunny day in Miami, Florida. Liza Parisaca, 9, pulls on a life vest and climbs into a sailboat. Today, the first-time sailor will learn how to steer the boat.

This isn't a family outing. It's gym class for students at Riverside Elementary School. It is one of many United States schools that have begun adding fun, new activities to gym class.

A new kind of physical education helps kids find workouts they can enjoy all their lives. The activities include yoga, kickboxing, cycling, dance, and even sailing.

Older gym programs often appealed to the best athletes. The new P.E. is for everyone. "Kids should never feel like they aren't good in gym," says Jayne Greenberg of the Miami School District.

A new report by the Institute of Medicine said that kids and adults should exercise an hour a day. But fewer than one in four kids gets even 20 minutes a day of intense exercise.

The United States government is trying to get kids moving. It started a program called *Verb: It's What You Do*. Greenberg says that for kids, the key to fitness is to have fun. "We want kids to find something they can enjoy for a lifetime," she says.

The New Gym (cont.)

Directions: Answer these questions. You may look at the article.

1. Where does Liza Parisaca go to school?

   a. Riverside, California

   b. Miami, Florida

   c. Washington, D.C.

2. What did Liza get to do in her new gym class?

   a. She learned how to sail.

   b. She learned how to kickbox.

   c. She learned yoga.

3. Why are school districts adding fun, new activities to gym class?

   _____

4. What are some other examples of activities for gym class that would be fun ways for kids to stay active?

   _____

   _____

5. How much time should kids and adults exercise every day? How much time do you exercise most days?

   _____

   _____

6. What is the name of the government program to get kids to exercise more? Why do you think they chose that name?

   _____

   _____

7. Do you enjoy exercising? Name one kind of exercise that you do not enjoy and one thing that you love to do. What makes the two activities different?

   _____

   _____

The New Gym (cont.)

Directions: Look at the chart and answer the questions.

Regular physical activity throughout life is important for maintaining a healthy body. This chart shows how many kids and adults exercise as much as experts recommend. The bars at the right show the targets for the year 2010.

Participation in Regular Physical Activity

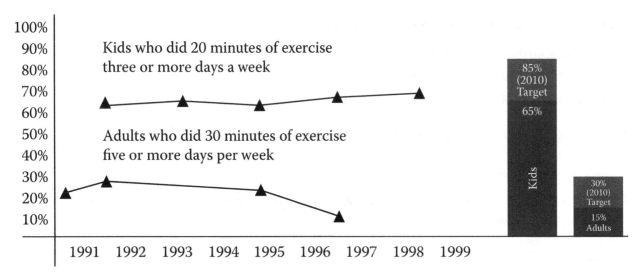

1. What percentage of kids exercised regularly in 1991? What percentage of adults exercised regularly that same year?

   _____

   _____

2. Are kids or adults doing better when it comes to exercising as much as they should?

   _____

   _____

3 What are the goals for both groups in 2010? Do you think either group will be able to make those goals? Explain your answer.

   _____

   _____

Alabama's New Coin

On March 24, Governor Bob Riley gave a shiny new quarter to every child who visited Helen Keller's birthplace in Tuscumbia, Alabama. The governor was celebrating his state's new quarter!

The coin features an image of Keller, who was blind and deaf. She overcame her disabilities and helped others to do the same. Keller's image was chosen from thousands of ideas submitted by Alabama schoolchildren. "Having her image on a national coin will remind us all of her courage and strength," said Governor Riley. Keller is the first blind person to be featured on United States money.

Alabama is the 22nd state to be celebrated in the 50 State Quarters Program. Alabama's quarter is the first United States coin to have Braille. That's a system of writing for the blind that uses raised dots.

Alabama's New Coin (cont.)

Directions: Answer these questions. You may look at the article.

1. How did Alabama's governor celebrate the state's new quarter?

    a. He handed out coins to every child visiting Helen Keller's home.

    b. He chose the image that would appear on the coin.

    c. He visited schools to hand out quarters.

2. Who suggested putting Helen Keller's image on the state quarter?

    a. Governor Riley

    b. Helen Keller's family

    c. Alabama schoolchildren

3. What disabilities did Helen Keller have?

    _____

4. Why was Helen Keller's image chosen for the state quarter? What makes that so special?

    _____

    _____

5. Why do you think it was decided to put Braille on the coin? How do you think Helen Keller would feel about this if she were alive today?

    _____

    _____

6. Do you think all United States money should have Braille? Why or why not?

    _____

    _____

7. How many other state quarters have you seen or collected? Do you think the state quarter program is a good idea? Why or why not?

    _____

    _____

    _____

Alabama's New Coin (cont.)

Directions: Look at the quarters. Answer the questions.

State Quarters

1. Which state quarter do you think was the first one to be launched? Why do you think that?

   _____

2. California was admitted into the Union in 1850. What year was Texas admitted?

   _____

3. What do you think the symbols on the Washington state quarter represent?

   _____

   _____

4. If your city or town could get its own quarter, what would you like to see on it? Why would you choose that image to represent the place where you live?

   _____

   _____

Nancy Wexler

Nancy Wexler is a scientist whose work has made history. She studies an illness called Huntington's Disease. It is an illness that affects the brain.

When she was 21, Wexler learned that her mother was dying from Huntington's. The disease runs in families, but its cause was a mystery. Wexler wanted to solve it. In 1972, she learned of villages in South America where almost everyone had the disease. She went there to study the people. Many scientists did not think she would find anything useful. But her work led doctors to discover how diseases that run in families are passed on from generation to generation. Now, she's helping to search for a cure.

"We shouldn't say, 'This is impossible!'" says Wexler. "We should say, 'It's possible,' and figure out how to do it."

Nancy Wexler *(cont.)*

Directions: Answer these questions. You may look at the article.

1. What is Wexler's job?

   a. She is a pilot.

   b. She is a scientist.

   c. She is a history teacher.

2. Why did Wexler decide to study Huntington's Disease?

   a. Wexler was suffering from the disease.

   b. Her father was suffering from the disease.

   c. Her mother was suffering from the disease.

3. Where did Wexler go to study the disease?

   _____

4. Why did she think she would find clues about the disease there?

   _____

   _____

5. What did Wexler's work lead to?

   _____

   _____

6. If the disease is passed from generation to generation, what might that mean for Wexler and her family?

   _____

   _____

7. If the disease had not affected Wexler's family, do you still think she would have studied it? Why or why not?

   _____

   _____

   _____

Nancy Wexler (cont.)

Directions: Look at the diagram. Answer the questions.

cerebrum
The largest part of the brain, the cerebrum controls movement, speech, intelligence, memory and emotion

thalamus
Processes sensory messages, such as touch, received from the body

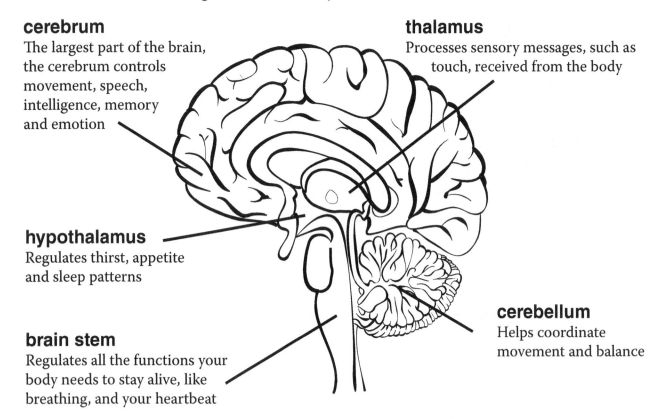

hypothalamus
Regulates thirst, appetite and sleep patterns

cerebellum
Helps coordinate movement and balance

brain stem
Regulates all the functions your body needs to stay alive, like breathing, and your heartbeat

1. Which part of the brain helps you remember what you study in school?

   _____

2. Which part of the brain makes sure you eat when you are hungry and rest when you are tired?

   _____

3. Why do you think there are laws that require you to wear a helmet when you ride a bike? What do you think might happen if you hit your head on the ground?

   _____

   _____

One Weird Dinosaur!

Imagine a small dinosaur light enough to glide from tree to tree. Now imagine it with four wings! Scientists have proof that such a creature existed. They recently found six fossils of the dinosaur in northeast China.

The odd dinosaur was about two and a half feet long. It lived about 130 million years ago. It had feathered-wings on each of its four limbs. Even its long tail was covered in feathers.

The dinosaur has been named *Microraptor gui*. It probably did not fly by flapping its wings. Scientists believe it used both sets of wings for gliding, moving the way flying squirrels do. Still, researchers believe the creature is related to modern birds.

Scientists are amazed by the strange fossil. "It would be a total oddity—the weirdest creature in the world of dinosaurs and birds," said Luis Chiappe of the Natural History Museum of Los Angeles County in California.

One Weird Dinosaur! *(cont.)*

Directions: Answer these questions. You may look at the article.

1. What makes this dinosaur so unusual?

   a. It was only two and a half feet long.

   b. It had a long tail.

   c. It had feathered-wings and was able to glide through the air.

2. What animal do scientists think this dinosaur was related to?

   a. They think the dinosaur was related to amphibians.

   b. They think the dinosaur was related to birds.

   c. They think the dinosaur was related to apes.

3. How do scientists know that this creature existed?

   _____

4. How long ago do scientists think it lived?

   _____

5. How does the story explain how the dinosaur flew? What animal does it compare its movements to?

   _____

   _____

6. Who is Luis Chiappe?

   _____

7. Chiappe called the dinosaur a "total oddity." What does that mean? What else did he say that describes it for the reader?

   _____

   _____

One Weird Dinosaur! (cont.)

Directions: Look at the chart. Answer the questions.

They Have So Much in Common!

Microraptor	Bird
Feathers	Feathers
Light frame for quick moving	Light, hollow bones allowing it to fly
Long, thin shoulder blades	Long, thin shoulder blades
Curved bones in the leg allow the feet to fold against the lower leg	Curved bones allow the feet to fold against the lower leg
Three-clawed feet—the middle claw is longest	Three-clawed feet—the middle claw is longest
Legs and feet built for two-legged walking These dinos had arms but walked only on their hind legs. Like birds, they had three forward-pointing toes	Legs and feet built for two-legged walking

1. How did this chart help you to better understand the article?

   _____

   _____

2. The chart points out all the similarities between the microraptor and the bird. What are two differences?

   _____

   _____

3. Which do you think is the biggest similarity between the two? Explain your answer.

   _____

   _____

Wild Rides

If you've ever been on a roller coaster, you know what it's like: You go up, you go down (boy, do you go down!), maybe you go upside down. Then before you know it, it's over. But as ride designers learn new tricks, coasters are getting faster, bigger, and wilder. This year's new rides are the wildest ever!

The first true roller coaster in America was built at Coney Island in New York City in 1884. It rolled along at six miles per hour. Now, coasters can reach speeds of 100 miles per hour! How did they get so fast? Computers.

Before engineers build a new roller coaster, they make a computer model that shows how it will run. This helps them make it as safe—and scary—as possible. Allan Schilke is one of the best-known ride designers in the world. He created the ride called *X*. Computers help him figure out how fast the riders can safely go. "There are limits that you don't go over, because you can break a bone," says Schilke. Yikes!

Most riders have no clue about how coasters are created. They're just along for the ride. Joey Stilphen, 13, of Bay Village, Ohio, tried out the *Wicked Twister* at Cedar Point last week. His verdict: "It's awesome!"

Wild Rides (cont.)

Directions: Answer these questions. You may look at the article.

1. How fast did the first roller coaster in the United States go?

    a. It traveled eight miles per hour.

    b. It traveled 100 miles per hour.

    c. It traveled six miles per hour.

2. How do engineers build new rides to make sure they are safe?

    a. They first build small models.

    b. They build computer models.

    c. They ask riders to submit designs.

3. Why do rides need speed limits, according to Allan Schilke?

    _____

4. How fast can the new roller coasters go?

    _____

5. Would you be willing to be the first person to ride on a new roller coaster? Why or why not?

    _____

    _____

    _____

6. Do you think designing roller coasters would be an interesting job? Why or why not?

    _____

    _____

    _____

Wild Rides *(cont.)*

Directions: Look at the chart. Answer the questions.

Top 5 States For Roller Coasters

Americans are crazy for roller coasters! The United States is home to 648 roller coasters, almost three times as many as any other country. Buckle your seat belt, and check out the states with the most operating coasters:

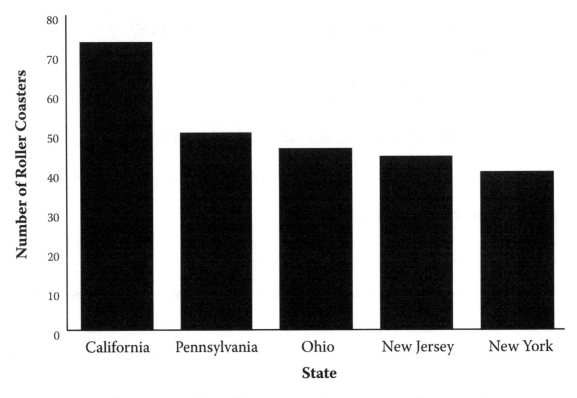

1. How many more roller coasters does California have than New York?

_____

2. Why do you think California has the most roller coasters?

_____

3. Why do you think so many people enjoy going on roller coasters and other wild rides? Explain your answer.

_____

_____

_____

Susan B. Anthony

Susan B. Anthony was born in 1820. In the 1800s, American women were not allowed to vote. She spent her life speaking out and fighting to change that.

Anthony attended every United States Congress from 1869 to 1906 to ask for an amendment to the Constitution. She died in 1906, before her dream came true. The 19th Amendment passed in 1920. It protects women's right to vote.

In 1979, the United States Mint created a Susan B. Anthony dollar coin. She is the first woman to appear on United States money.

Susan B. Anthony (cont.)

Directions: Answer these questions. You may look at the article.

1. What did Susan B. Anthony fight for?

   a. She fought for a seat on Congress.

   b. She fought for women's right to vote.

   c. She fought for the right to appear on a U.S coin.

2. How did she try to change the Constitution?

   a. She passed an amendment.

   b. She ran for Congress.

   c. She attended every Congress for 37 years to ask for an amendment.

3. Why do you think women were not allowed to vote in the 1800s?

   _____

   _____

4. What does the 19th Amendment do?

   _____

   _____

5. How many years passed between the time Anthony died and the time the 19th Amendment passed?

   _____

   _____

6. Besides creating a dollar coin for her, what else do you think would be a good tribute for Anthony?

   _____

   _____

7. How do you think Anthony would feel about all the women leaders today?

   _____

   _____

Susan B. Anthony (cont.)

Directions: Look at the pictures. Answer the questions.

Commemorative Coins

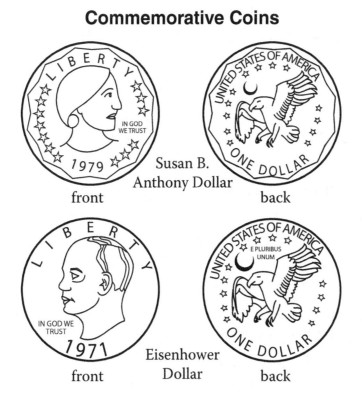

Susan B.
Anthony Dollar

front   back

Eisenhower
Dollar

front   back

1. List three things that are different about these dollar coins.

   _____

   _____

2. List three things that are the same about the coins.

   _____

   _____

3. What are three things that designers have to think about when they create a new
   United States coin?

   _____

   _____

The Paws That Heal

Sounds of laughter echo from a room at the UCLA Medical Center. It's a two-year-old patient laughing. She's watching Corky, a tiny Yorkshire Terrier, roll over and dance. "I want him in my bed!" shouts the six-year-old in the room next door.

Corky is just one of 40 dogs making the rounds at the huge hospital in Los Angeles, California. Every dog wears a picture identification card and a blue scarf with a paw-print design.

In hospitals around the country, dogs are helping patients get better. Most of the dogs are trained by Therapy Dogs International in New Jersey or the Delta Society in Seattle, Washington. According to Delta, 4,500 "pet partners" have helped 350,000 patients in 45 states.

UCLA's program began in 1994. Before joining the pack, the 40 dogs at UCLA had to pass a test to prove they were gentle enough for the job. Si'ska, a big German Shepherd, surely must have passed with flying colors. She flops on heart patient Daniel Uribe's bed and lovingly nuzzles him. "She is life," Uribe says. "Like sun and air."

The Paws That Heal (cont.)

Directions: Answer these questions. You may look at the article.

1. What is this story about?

   a. The story is about UCLA Medical Center.

   b. The story is about Corky, the therapy dog.

   c. The story is about how dogs are helping hospital patients feel better.

2. How do hospital employees know these dogs are allowed to be there?

   a. The trainers have special permission letters.

   b. The dogs have ID cards and paw-print scarves.

   c. The dogs wear special T-shirts.

3. What do you think it is about dogs that make some patients feel better?

   _____

   _____

4. Do you think therapy dogs work for every kind of hospital patient? Explain your answer.

   _____

   _____

5. How many "pet partners" have been trained across the United States?

   _____

6. How many patients have they helped?

   _____

7. Why do you think dogs were chosen for this kind of program? Can you think of another animal that might be good at helping hospital patients? Explain your answer.

   _____

   _____

The Paws That Heal (cont.)

Directions: Look at the chart. Answer the questions.

Rules for Participating in the Pet Partners Therapy Animal Program

Animals Must	Owners Must
Live in the owner's home for at least one year	Be at least 16 years old
Be at least one year old	Successfully pass the Pet Partners Program Course
Be friendly	Have good control of the animal
Be healthy	
Be well groomed	

1. Why do you think the program has rules like these?

   _____

   _____

2. How old does the animal's owner need to be in order to participate in the program? Do you think this is fair? Explain your answer.

   _____

   _____

3. Do you think there should be rules for the patients who visit with the dogs, too? If so, what rules would you have for them?

   _____

   _____

#50242—Comprehension and Critical Thinking

Fighting Hunger

Catherine Bertini has 90 million mouths to feed. She has traveled the world as chief of the United Nations World Food Program (WFP) for nine years. She is responsible for raising money and "making sure food gets to the right people at the right time." She is the first American and the first woman to head the WFP. The WFP brings food to people in very poor nations.

Bertini grew up in Cortland, New York. Now she lives in Rome, Italy, where the WFP is based.

One of her goals has been to make certain that hungry women and children get fed. Bertini says she has the job of a lifetime. "In how many places," she asks, "do you get to improve the lives of millions of people?"

Fighting Hunger (cont.)

Directions: Answer these questions. You may look at the article.

1. What does the WFP do?

    a. It runs a chain of grocery stores.

    b. It raises money for poor people.

    c. It helps feed people in poor countries.

2. Where did Catherine Bertini grow up?

    a. Rome, Italy

    b. Cortland, New York

    c. Washington, D.C.

3. What does the story mean when it says that Bertini has "90 million mouths" to feed?

    _____

    _____

4. Why do you think that raising money is a big part of her job?

    _____

    _____

5. Why do you think so many people around the world have a hard time getting food?

    _____

    _____

6. What do you think would happen if organizations like WFP did not exist?

    _____

    _____

7. How can you tell how Bertini feels about her job?

    _____

    _____

Fighting Hunger (cont.)

Directions: Look at the map. Answer the questions.

Hunger "Hot Spots" in Africa

1. What do you think a hunger "hot spot" is?

   _____

   _____

2. What kinds of problems do you think they have in Africa that create so many hunger problems? Do you think any of these problems exist in the United States?

   _____

   _____

   _____

Fantasies in Ice

What do you get when you mix snow, ice, and bitter cold with a heaping shovelful of imagination? A winter celebration with sparkling sculptures and lots of frozen fun!

Some of the world's coldest cities follow this recipe every winter with great success. The Ice Lantern Festival in Harbin, China, welcomes a million visitors a year. The ice sculptures are so stunning that folks don't mind the -20°F temperatures.

Ice carving is an ancient Chinese tradition. Recently, an exhibit celebrating Chinese ice art opened in The Hague, the Netherlands. In Sapporo, Japan, artists work in snow. Giant snowy sculptures attract tourists from around the world.

Visitors to Canada's Winter Carnival in Quebec can stay at the nearby Ice Hotel, where it's 26°F inside! The hotel is made of 250 tons of ice and 5,000 tons of snow. Even the beds are made of ice. *Brrrr!*

Fantasies in Ice (cont.)

Directions: Answer these questions. You may look at the article.

1. Where is the Ice Lantern Festival held each year?

   a. Ontario, Canada
   b. Harbin, China
   c. Detroit, Michigan

2. How much ice is used to build the Ice Hotel in Quebec, Canada?

   a. 50 tons
   b. 5,000 tons
   c. 250 tons

3. Why do you think a million people visit the Ice Lantern Festival every year?

   _____

   _____

4. How do you think artists learn to make ice sculptures?

   _____

   _____

5. Would you ever want to stay in the Ice Hotel? Why or why not?

   _____

   _____

6. What are some other events or activities you think might take place at winter festivals? Describe an event or contest that could only happen at a carnival where there was lots of snow and ice.

   _____

   _____

7. Do you like really cold or really hot weather best? Which weather do you like better when you go on vacation? Explain your answer.

   _____

   _____

Fantasies in Ice (cont.)

Directions: Look at the pictures. Answer the questions.

1. In what ways are these two hotel rooms similar?

   _____

   _____

2. In what ways are they different?

   _____

   _____

3. Which one would you rather stay in while you are on vacation? Why?

   _____

   _____

Meet a Dino Hunter

Ever since she was little, Sue Hendrickson has been in a good position to find hidden treasures. "I was shy and walked with my head down," she says. "But my curiosity was strong." She turned her curiosity and talent for finding things into an exciting job. Now she is a famous fossil hunter.

In August 1990 she uncovered one of the largest and most complete T-Rex fossils ever found. "It took 67 million years, but we finally got to it," she says.

When she's not digging for bones, Hendrickson dives in search of sunken treasure. She lives a life full of adventure. She hopes other girls will follow in her path. "Volunteer out in the field with professionals," she says. "And focus on school. It will train you to learn on your own."

Meet a Dino Hunter *(cont.)*

Directions: Answer these questions. You may look at the article.

1. Why was Sue Hendrickson in a good position to find hidden treasures?
   a. She walked with her head down, and she was curious.
   b. She knew where treasures were hidden.
   c. She liked to dig in the ground.

2. Why does she say it is important to focus on school?
   a. It is important so you have something to do during the day.
   b. It is important to have time to play with friends.
   c. It is important to train you to learn on your own.

3. Why did Sue Hendrickson think she would be a good fossil hunter?

   _____

   _____

4. What was one of her most important discoveries?

   _____

   _____

5. Since they no longer exist, how do we know about dinosaurs?

   _____

   _____

6. Why would Sue Hendrickson be a good role model for young girls?

   _____

   _____

7. Would you rather dig for dinosaur bones or dive for sunken treasures? Explain your answer.

   _____

   _____

Meet a Dino Hunter (cont.)

Directions: Look at the picture. Answer the question.

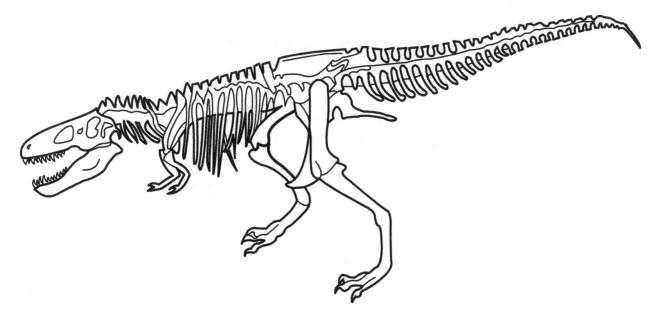

This T-Rex, on display at The Field Museum in Chicago, is named "Sue"—that is for Sue Hendrickson, the fossil hunter who found her. It is 41 feet long and stands 13 feet tall at the hips.

If you were writing a letter to Sue Hendrickson to ask about her fossil-hunting job and discovery of the T-Rex fossil, what would you write? What kind of questions would you ask?

Dear Ms. Hendrickson,

_____

_____

_____

_____

_____

_____

A Master Illustrator

"Just look at these muscles. I must be the strongest man in the world," boasts Shadusa in *Master Man,* the newest book by artist David Wisniewski. The story comes from a folktale told by the Hausa people of Nigeria, Africa.

Wisniewski created the book's illustrations in his usual style: layers of cut pieces of paper. One design can have up to 20 different layers and take up to five days to create! Because his art takes so long to complete, Wisniewski only works on stories he likes. What he likes best is to make people laugh. Wisniewski is trained to do just that. He was once a circus clown! Says Wisniewski: "I use everything I know to create my books."

While some of his books are funny, they also have strong messages. His award-winning book *Golem* is about a clay figure brought to life to help the Jewish people. "The lesson in *Master Man* is, don't brag," says Wisniewski. "But I don't like to preach. I'm an entertainer."

A Master Illustrator (cont.)

Directions: Answer these questions. You may look at the article.

1. How does David Wisniewski create his book's illustrations?

   a. He uses pen and ink.

   b. He uses layers of cut pieces of paper.

   c. He uses crayons and paints.

2. How did Wisniewski become trained to make people laugh?

   a. He was once a circus clown.

   b. He read books about comedy.

   c. He took comedy classes.

3. What is the message of the book Master Man?

   a. The message is do not lie.

   b. The message is do not brag.

   c. The message is do not steal.

4. Why does David Wisniewski's artwork take a long time to complete?

   _____

   _____

5. If you were illustrating your own book, what method of artwork would you use? Use details to explain your answer.

   _____

   _____

6. Why does David Wisniewski consider himself an entertainer?

   _____

   _____

7. Would you like to read one of David Wisniewski's books? Why or why not?

   _____

   _____

A Master Illustrator (cont.)

Directions: Look at the medals and read the descriptions. Answer the questions.

The Randolph Caldecott Medal

The Caldecott Medal was named in honor of 19th-century English illustrator Randolph Caldecott. The American Library Association awards it each year to the artist of the most distinguished American picture book for children.

The John Newbery Medal

The Newbery Medal was named for 18th-century British bookseller John Newbery. The American Library Association awards it each year to the author of the most distinguished contribution to American literature for children.

1. Which award did David Wisniewski win? How do you know?

   _____

2. Do you think that one book should be allowed to win both awards? Why or why not?

   _____

   _____

3. Do you ever look at a book's cover to see if it has won either of these awards? Do you think that might be a good way to decide whether to read a book? Explain your answer.

   _____

   _____

References Cited

Grigg, W. S., M. C. Daane, Y. Jin, and J. R. Campbell. 2003. National assessment of educational progress. The nation's report card: Reading 2002. Washington, DC: U.S. Department of Education.

Gulek, C. 2003. Preparing for high-stakes testing. *Theory into Practice* 42 (1): 42–50.

Ivey, G., and K. Broaddus. 2000. Tailoring the fit: Reading instruction and middle school readers. *The Reading Teacher* 54 (1): 68–78.

Kletzien, S. B. 1998. Information text or narrative text? Children's preferences revisited. Paper presented at the National Reading Conference, Austin, TX.

Miller, D. 2002. *Reading with meaning: Teaching comprehension in the primary grades.* Portland, ME: Stenhouse.

Moss, B. and J. Hendershot. 2002. Exploring sixth graders' selection of nonfiction trade books. *The Reading Teacher* 56 (1): 6–18.

Pardo, L. S. 2002. Book club for the twenty-first century. *Illinois Reading Council Journal* 30 (4): 14–23.

RAND Reading Study Group. 2002. Reading for understanding: Toward a research and development program in reading comprehension. Santa Monica, CA: Office of Education Research and Improvement.

U.S. Congress. House. *No Child Left Behind Act of 2001.* Pub. L. No. 107–110, 115 Stat. 1425 (2002).

Student Achievement Graph

Passage Title	# of Questions	Number of Questions Correctly Answered						
		1	2	3	4	5	6	7

Answer Key

Many of the answers will show an example of how the students might respond. For many of the questions there may be more than one correct answer.

Page 19
1. c
2. b
3. It was 33 feet long, had teeth the size of bananas, and backbones as wide as dinner plates.
4. Scientists say that no one knew about this kind of sea creature before.
5. Yes, because its teeth were so big.
6. The bones were found in the Arctic Ocean. Similar bones were found in Britain, Germany, and Russia.
7. They will be able to compare the bones they find in other places to the bones in this complete skeleton.

Page 20
1. Answers will vary.
2. Answers will vary.

Page 22
1. b
2. c
3. She used sign language and Braille.
4. She helped other blind people around the world.
5. Answers will vary.
6. Answers will vary.

Page 23
1. touch; answers will vary
2. Answers will vary.

Page 23 (cont.)
3. Answers will vary.

Page 25
1. c
2. b
3. He took photos, made careful notes, and collected feathers.
4. Answers will vary.
5. They take notes and photos to observe differences in particular birds so they can tell them apart. Answers will vary.
6. (Students will draw a picture.)

Page 26
1. Answers will vary.
2. Answers will vary.

Page 28
1. b
2. a
3. Answers will vary.
4. one year
5. It made racial discrimination in public places against the law.
6. Answers will vary.

Page 29
1. Answer will depend on current year.
2. 41 years
3. Answers will vary.

Page 31
1. b
2. c

Page 31 (cont.)
3. gorillas, chimpanzees, bonobos, and orangutans
4. The countries are very poor. People in these countries need food and jobs.
5. It would be a great loss if these animals became extinct; answers will vary.
6. He is with the Wildlife Conservation Society.
7. Answers will vary.

Page 32
1. Both apes eat leaves and fruit. Both are covered in hair.
2. color of hair, where it lives; answers will vary.
3. The orangutan's hook-shaped hands and feet probably help it grab tree branches.

Page 34
1. c
2. b
3. He wrote and illustrated *Kamishibai Man*.
4. He does watercolor paintings.
5. He grew up in Japan.
6. Answers will vary.
7. Answers will vary.

Page 35
Student will write a short story.

Answer Key (cont.)

Page 37

1. b
2. c
3. Kids collect sap from trees; visit the school pond; pick up trash; clean the school's chicken coop; study the life cycles of plants and animals; draw sketches of the things they see outdoors; keep track of changes from season to season (only four items necessary).
4. The walls and floors are made with recycled material.
5. Answers will vary.
6. Answers will vary.
7. Answers will vary.

Page 38

1. Answers will vary.
2. Answers will vary.
3. Answers will vary.

Page 40

1. c
2. b
3. They studied hair samples, dentures, eyeglasses, and clothing.
4. 19, 45, 57; they want to show him at the major stages of his life; answers will vary.
5. They probably respect Washington and feel like they know him personally; they want visitors to his home to get a better sense of who he was; answers will vary.

Page 40 (cont.)

6. Answers will vary.

Page 41

1. 3; answers will vary
2. He is taking the oath of office.
3. Answers will vary.

Page 43

1. b
2. a
3. They want to help protect the elephants.
4. 20; that is 14 more than it has now
5. They are hunted for their ivory tusks and meat; destruction of natural resources like vegetation and water make it hard for them to survive; clearing of forests and logging are destroying their habitat. Answers will vary.
6. Answers will vary.
7. Dwindle means to shrink or decrease.

Page 44

1. one million
2. about 450,000 (between 300,000 and 600,000, according to the passage)
3. They may become extinct.
4. Answers will vary.

Page 46

1. c
2. a
3. She wanted to educate kids about the contribution of civil rights leaders.
4. Atlanta, Georgia

Page 46 *(cont.)*

5. Inductees will come from all over the world.
6. 17; about 600
7. Answers will vary.

Page 47

1. two; no death date is given
2. Andrew Young; Thurgood Marshall
3. Not every honoree is an African American; people of all races played a part in the civil rights movement. Answers will vary.

Page 49

1. b
2. a
3. a bike shop
4. They played with kites and a flying toy. Both toys have to do with flying. Answers will vary.
5. the wings and propellers
6. Answers will vary.

Page 50

1. All have wings; all have landing wheels (answers will vary). The Boeing does not have a propeller; it is much bigger and could fly much faster than the other two. Answers will vary.
2. So people can travel more safely and faster; answers will vary.
3. Boeing 747

Page 52

1. c
2. b
3. Answers will vary.

Answer Key (cont.)

Page 52 (cont.)

4. Answers will vary.

5. Answers will vary.

6. Answers will vary.

Page 53

1. They are at a park. They are playing basketball, climbing on the jungle gym, jumping rope, and riding bikes. Answers will vary.

2. Answers will vary.

3. Answers will vary.

Page 55

1. b

2. c

3. The Nobel Peace Prize is one of the biggest honors in the world. It is given each year to the world's top peacemaker.

4. She cried because she was so happy and proud of her daughter.

5. She meant that she had dreamed of achieving what her daughter was able to accomplish.

6. Answers will vary.

Page 56

1. six

2. physics and chemistry; both are awards for science achievements

3. The prize in literature is for great books. The medal looks like someone being told a story (answers will vary).

4. It looks like three people being brought together.

Page 58

1. b

2. c

3. elephants and antelopes

4. They found out that male baboons take care of their own babies. Researchers had previously thought that baboon dads didn't even know which babies were theirs.

5. Male baboons identify their young by look and smell.

6. The baby would probably die; answers will vary.

7. Joan Silk is a college teacher who worked on the study. She compares male baboons to humans.

Page 59

1. Answers will vary.

2. Answers will vary.

3. Answers will vary.

Page 61

1. b

2. c

3. The No Child Left Behind Act; answers will vary

4. Answers will vary.

5. Answers will vary.

6. Answers will vary.

Page 62

1. Answers will vary.

2. Answers will vary.

3. Answers will vary.

Page 64

1. a

2. c

Page 64 (cont.)

3. Brown versus Board of Education of Topeka

4. Black and white children went to separate public schools.

5. Answers will vary.

6. He was the first black person to serve on the United States Supreme Court.

7. two years

Page 65

1. 34 years

2. William Rehnquist

3. William Rehnquist and John Marshall Harlan

Page 67

1. b

2. c

3. About 31 million people visited children's museums last year. In 1991, the number of visitors was about 10 million.

4. Baltimore's Port Discovery Museum in Maryland

5. You can dig for dinosaur fossils, play musical instruments, and build machines.

6. Answers will vary.

7. Answers will vary.

Page 68

1. They are at a children's museum. They are digging in sand for dinosaur fossils; looking at bugs through telescopes; and creating mobiles with origami.

Answer Key (cont.)

Page 68 (cont.)

2. Answers will vary.

3. Answers will vary.

Page 70

1. b

2. a

3. It caused a problem because it is a predator and has no enemies in the United States. United States wildlife officials poisoned the lake to stop the spread of the species in the United States.

4. Most travel into the country with humans on boats or planes.

5. Answers will vary.

6. Answers will vary.

Page 71

1. New Jersey or Illinois; answers will vary

2. The beetles probably came into the country in a single place and have been spreading slowly.

3. Trees all over the country will be harmed or die if we do not stop the spread of the beetle.

Page 73

1. b

2. a

3. School districts are trying to get kids to find workouts they can enjoy all their lives.

4. Answers will vary.

5. one hour per day; answers will vary

Page 73 (cont.)

6. It is called *Verb: It's What You Do*. Officials probably chose that name because a verb is an action word and the program is all about being active.

7. Answers will vary.

Page 74

1. Sixty-one percent of kids exercised regularly in 1991. Twenty-five percent of adults exercised regularly that same year.

2. A greater percentage of kids than adults are exercising the recommended amount.

3 The goal is for 85% of kids and 30% of adults to be exercising the recommended amounts in 2010; answers will vary.

Page 76

1. a

2. c

3. Helen Keller was blind and deaf.

4. Helen Keller's image was chosen for the state quarter to honor her courage and strength. Keller is the first blind person to be featured on United States money.

5. Braille was used on the coin so that blind people would be able to easily recognize it. Helen Keller would probably be very proud of this honor. (Answers will vary.)

Page 76 (cont.)

6. Answers will vary.

7. Answers will vary.

Page 77

1. Delaware; it says "the first state" on the quarter

2. Texas was admitted in 1845.

3. The mountain is Mount Rainier, an active volcano in Washington. The fish is a salmon, which has provided nourishment for the native peoples of the Pacific Northwest. Washington is nicknamed the "Evergreen State" because of its many lush evergreen forests. (Answers will vary.)

4. Answers will vary.

Page 79

1. b

2. c

3. She went to South American villages.

4. She thought she would find clues about the disease because almost everyone in these villages had it.

5. Her work led doctors to discover how diseases that run in families are passed on from generation to generation.

6. It might mean that Wexler and her family will get the disease.

7. Answers will vary.

Answer Key *(cont.)*

Page 81
1. cerebrum
2. hypothalamus
3. There are helmet laws to protect people from getting head injuries. Head injuries sometimes result in brain injuries, which can affect your bodily functions, your speech, movement, memory, and intelligence. (Answers will vary.)

Page 82
1. c
2. b
3. Scientists recently found six fossils of the dinosaur in northeast China.
4. 130 million years ago
5. Scientists believe it used its wings for gliding, moving the way flying squirrels do.
6. Luis Chiappe is a scientist at the Natural History Museum of Los Angeles County in California.
7. It means the dinosaur was extremely strange. Chiappe also said the dinosaur would have been "the weirdest creature in the world of dinosaurs and birds."

Page 83
1. Answers will vary.
2. Answers will vary.
3. Answers will vary.

Page 85
1. c
2. b
3. If you go over certain limits, you can break a bone, Schilke says.
4. 100 miles per hour
5. Answers will vary.
6. Answers will vary.

Page 86
1. about 35
2. California has the largest population.
3. Answers will vary.

Page 88
1. b
2. c
3. In the 1800s, women did not have the same rights as men. They had no political power or economic independence. Only men who owned property could vote.
4. The 19th Amendment protects women's right to vote.
5. 14 years
6. Answers will vary.
7. Answers will vary.

Page 89
1. Answers may include: the person featured; the year; stars on front of Anthony coin; edges of Anthony coin are not smooth (choose three only).

Page 89 *(cont.)*
2. Answers may include: Both are about the same size; backs of coins are the same; Liberty, In God We Trust, and E Pluribus Unum appear on both (choose three only).
3. Answers may include: Designers must consider the size, shape, and weight of the coin, who should be featured and what their image should look like, and what should appear on the back on the coin (choose three only).

Page 91
1. c
2. b
3. Dogs probably calm patients down and take their minds off their pain and fear of being ill. (Answers will vary.)
4. Therapy dogs probably work best for patients who like dogs and who are able to sit up and play with them. (Answers will vary.)
5. There are 4,500 "pet partners."
6. They have helped 350,000 patients nationwide.
7. Dogs were probably chosen because most people feel comfortable with them and they can be easily trained. Answers will vary.

Answer Key (cont.)

Page 92

1. The rules are for the safety of the patients and the dogs; answers will vary.

2. 16; answers will vary

3. Answers might include that the patients should have to be gentle with the dogs (answers will vary).

Page 94

1. c

2. b

3. It means that there are about 90 million poor people in the world who need help getting food from the WFP.

4. It costs a lot of money to get food to people all over the world.

5. War, disease, extreme poverty, and natural disasters are just a few reasons why so many people around the world have a hard time getting food.

6. If organizations like WFP didn't exist, many people around the world would die of starvation.

7. You can tell that Bertini loves her job and feels proud about what she does because she says, "In how many places do you get to improve the lives of millions of people?"

Page 95

1. A hunger "hot spot" is where the hunger problem has become a crisis and many people are at risk of dying of starvation.

2. Many people are too poor to buy or grow food; conflicts and war have made it hard to get food to people; drought and bad weather make it hard to grow crops. Poverty and natural disasters exist in the United States, creating hunger problems in some areas.

Page 97

1. b

2. c

3. The ice sculptures are so beautiful; answers will vary

4. They learn from tradition being passed down; they practice with snow and ice; answers will vary.

5. Answers will vary.

6. Answers will vary.

7. Answers will vary.

Page 98

1. Both rooms have beds. Both are used for people to stay in while on vacation.

2. In one room, the bed is a regular mattress; the other has a bed made of ice. In one, the temperature in the room is 74°F, and in the other, it is 26°F.

3. Answers will vary.

Page 100

1. a

2. c

3. She had a curiosity and talent for finding things.

4. She uncovered one of the largest and most complete T-Rex fossils.

5. We have dinosaur fossils to learn from.

6. Even though most fossil hunters are men, she showed that women can achieve their dreams with hard work and dedication. (Answers will vary.)

7. Answers will vary.

Page 101

1. Reponses will vary.

Page 103

1. b

2. a

3. b

4. He uses layers of cut up pieces of paper for the illustrations.

5. Answers will vary.

6. He likes to write books that people can enjoy.

7. Answers will vary.

Page 104

1. The Caldecott Award; the article talks about his illustrations.

2. Answers will vary. (Books are allowed to win both awards.)

3. Answers will vary.